RENAISSANCE

THE REBIRTH AND RISE OF
DUQUESNE UNIVERSITY FOOTBALL

RENAISSANCE

THE REBIRTH AND RISE OF
DUQUESNE UNIVERSITY FOOTBALL

SAM COSTANZO

Copyright © 2025 by Sam Costanzo

All rights reserved. No part of this book may be reproduced or transmitted in any form without prior written permission except in the case of brief quotations embodied in critical articles and reviews.

Printed in the United States of America.

ISBN: 978-1-63385-553-3
Library of Congress Control Number: 2025913727

Published by
Word Association Publishers
205 Fifth Avenue
Tarentum, Pennsylvania 15084

www.wordassociation.com
1.800.827.7903

DEDICATION
BY SAM COSTANZO

To my beautiful wife, Barbara, whose unshakable loyalty and boundless love have been my greatest inspiration.

And to our children — Stef, Cindy, Sal and Suzie — whose laughter and joy light up our world and remind us daily of life's true magic.

Thank you for being an infinite source of motivation and happiness.

This book is dedicated to you with all my love and gratitude.

FOREWORD
BY SUZIE COSTANZO LACHUT

EVER SINCE I CAN REMEMBER, I have heard my Dad tell stories about building the football program at Duquesne. He cherishes these memories and shares them colorfully, always with enthusiasm, keen detail, and a fond and knowing smile. If you've been lucky enough to be in his company when he recounts his football days, you feel as though you were a part of them, too. Like his pride over securing Three Rivers Stadium as the home field for the Gridiron Dukes or selecting lifelong friend and mentor Dan McCann as the head coach.

These stories are more than just anecdotes, though. They represent a tremendous amount of effort, ingenuity, and drive — qualities I have always admired in my Dad. He built the football program brick by brick, firming up budget approval; hiring coaches; scheduling practice and playing time; securing field space; booking buses, flights and hotels for away games; and purchasing uniforms (to name a few). He achieved all of this while playing the game that he loved and that served as the foundation for much of his personal philosophy. Vince Lombardi was quoted as saying, "Football is a great deal like life in that it teaches that work, sacrifice, perseverance, competitive drive, selflessness and respect for authority is the price that each and every one of us must pay to achieve any goal that is worthwhile." If you know my Dad, there isn't a goal that he's set his mind to that he hasn't achieved. Bringing football back to the Bluff as a 19-year-old kid is a great example of that.

When we attended the celebration of the Duquesne Dukes football team winning the 2023 NEC Championship this spring, I couldn't help but think of my Dad as a young man, eager to restore football on campus after a 19-year hiatus. Had he not possessed the industriousness, resiliency and spirit of entrepreneurship it took to launch a successful club football program back in 1969, I doubt that these modern players would have had a chance to compete for a conference title today. I watched the young student athletes step up on the stage, accepting their conference championship rings, their faces full of pride and possibility. I imagined my Dad at their age, on our Bluff, channeling the full force of his will to create something that would go on to grow and thrive after 55 years. So few of us can claim such a powerful legacy. I wonder if young Sam Costanzo knew the enormous potential of his passion project. The charming kid from Blawnox, living on his beloved 13th floor of St. Martin's Hall. The one whom his friends dubbed, "Jacket and Tie Man" because of his business instincts and prowess for influencing and negotiating. No. 65, the defensive tackle, who by his own admission may have been slow on his first step — but was never once outworked on the field.

If the stories in this book of the early days of club football at Duquesne aren't impressive enough, consider that more than five decades later my Dad remains a booster, avid fan and advocate of Duquesne Athletics. In Italian, our family name Costanzo means "firm, constant, or steadfast." I'd challenge anyone to find a more steadfast supporter of the Duquesne Dukes and the University than my Dad. Whether you're a friend, alum, donor, supporter, or student, with this book you're welcomed to share in a piece of this rich history, too. I hope you enjoy reading it as much as I have. May it inspire you to listen to your instincts, to believe in yourself, and to build your dream.

SUZIE COSTANZO LACHUT
Duquesne University A'06, GA'08
August 2024

Sam Costanzo, the Club Football "jacket & tie man" today.

INTRODUCTION
BY KEN GORMLEY

THE DUQUESNE DUKES football legacy stands as a testament to resilience, student engagement, camaraderie and the indomitable pursuit of excellence on and off the field. From the very beginnings here on the Bluff, this University has encouraged student engagement and leadership in the classroom, in the community, and through athletic competition. Nowhere is student engagement and leadership more evident than in the story of the Duquesne Dukes football team. And there is no one better to tell the definitive history of the Dukes football program than esteemed alumnus and University Board Member Emeritus, Sam Costanzo, who remains dedicated to his alma mater and our athletics program.

The Dukes football team was a national powerhouse in the 1920s and '30s. They won two bowl games and were ranked among top teams in the nation — along with Alabama, Tennessee and Notre Dame. But World War II halted the program, which led to its discontinuation following the 1950 season. As you'll read in these pages, the rebirth of Duquesne's football program began in the winter of 1969. Visions of a new club program were brought to the University Athletic Committee, which, at that time, was comprised of two alums, two faculty members and two students. One of those students was Sam Costanzo. He and the committee voted unanimously to bring football back to life on the Bluff. Sam and a determined crew of fellow students had amazing foresight. The club football program they went on to establish in 1969 would bring the University notoriety and prestige — and would create vital opportunities for generations of student athletes.

In 1970, the second season, Costanzo made a decision that changed history: He and the crew of the 13th floor of St. Martin's Hall interviewed a number of coaches and selected Dan McCann, a former Pitt quarterback who coached the freshman team at North Catholic High School and had a 27-0 record. He asked McCann to be Duquesne's new coach. Led by Coach McCann, the Gridiron Dukes bounced from field to field, grinding out impressive wins against tough competitors. By the 1973 season, with the support of Allegheny County Commissioner Tom Foerster, the undefeated Gridiron Dukes arranged to play a championship game on the Steelers' home turf at Three Rivers Stadium. Members of the organizing committee also included iconic Steelers founder Art Rooney, who played football for Duquesne Prep School, and Father Henry McAnulty, then-president of the University. After a nail-biter of a game — with exciting plays by players like Rod Hess, Steve Sherer, Gary McHenry, John Stefanik, Terry Russell, Dave Thomas and Frank Hooper — the Gridiron Dukes beat #2 Mattatuck and brought home the championship trophy to the Bluff. With only 29 players on the team, everyone made a significant contribution.

The story of Duquesne football is a tale of student drive and initiative that has inspired generations of players, alumni and fans here on campus — and far beyond. It's the story of a dedicated, talented and often colorful cast of characters -- whom Sam brings to life vividly on these pages.

Sam Costanzo helps us to celebrate far more than touchdowns and victories, in producing this book. He honors the very essence of Duquesne's college football saga, from the club program's inaugural 1969 kickoff against Niagara University, to games played on the same hallowed turf where the "Immaculate Reception" took place — Three Rivers Stadium — to the program's transition to full intercollegiate status. As I write this introduction in 2024, our Dukes remain the reigning NEC champions — a title they earned with the same grit and determination they had back in the early 1970s.

We are forever indebted to Sam Costanzo — and all of the players, coaches and fans who contributed to making this story of grit and victory come to life — for helping us honor generations of Dukes who continue to proudly wear our Duquesne red and blue on the athletic field.

Go Dukes!

KEN GORMLEY
President, Duquesne University
August 2024

DUQUESNE CLUB FOOTBALL ROAD TO THE NATIONAL CHAMPIONSHIP

1969 Season — Won 2, Lost 4

OPPONENT	DU	OP
at Niagara	0	20
vs. St. Francis	33	0
vs. Fordham	0	36
at St. Vincent's	12	14
vs. Federal City	0	60
vs. St. Bonaventure	20	0

1970 Season — Won 4, Lost 3, Tied 1

OPPONENT	DU	OP
at Steubenville	41	6
at Loyola (Ill.)	40	12
vs. Niagara	6	6
at Fordham	0	12
vs. St. John's	6	41
vs. St. Vincent's	34	6
vs. King's	2	28
at St. Bonaventure	\multicolumn{2}{c}{*won by forfeit*}

1971 Season — Won 4, Lost 4

OPPONENT	DU	OP
vs. Steubenville	47	6
vs. St. Francis	41	13
at St. John's	12	35
vs. Loyola (Ill.)	27	28
at King's	12	27
at St. Vincent's	28	14
at Niagara	5	11
vs. Catholic	*won by forfeit*	

1972 Season — Won 7, Lost 1

OPPONENT	DU	OP
vs. Niagara	26	16
vs. Allegheny CC	29	0
vs. King's	16	12
at St. Francis	14	5
vs. Cleveland State	12	8
at Canisius	20	22
vs. St. Vincent's	44	0
vs. Steubenville	72	6

1973 Season — Won 10, Lost 0

OPPONENT	DU	OP
vs. Allegheny CC	22	0
at Niagara	34	0
vs. American	18	0
vs. St. Francis	14	3
at King's	26	15
vs. Catholic	18	0
vs. Canisius	23	0
at St. Vincent's	12	0
vs. Steubenville	*won by forfeit*	

NATIONAL CHAMPIONSHIP GAME

vs. Mattatuck CC	13	7

CONTENTS

    Dedication v
    Foreword vii
    Introduction xi
1 Rebooting Duquesne Football 1
2 All Hands on Deck 15
3 Robbing Peter to Pay Paul 21
4 Spreading the Word Beyond Campus in Those Early Days 25
5 Ready or Not 29
6 Coach Nicoletti Moves On 37
7 McCann Takes the Reins & Rod Hess's Catch 41
8 Club Football Is No Joke 61
9 Football Season 1971 65
10 Gridiron Dukes Take Giant Step Forward in 1972 71
11 Little Sammy From South Catholic 79
12 Setting the Stage for Championship Glory 83
13 The Monsters of Mattatuck 87
14 The National Championship Game 91
15 Celebration at the Pilot House…Then Goldstein's 101
16 Publicizing Duquesne's Club Football Team 105
17 Pete Kulyk 109
18 Through the Eyes of His Daughter 111
19 Born With Duquesne in His Blood 115
20 A Tip of the Cap From Head Coach Jerry Schmitt 119
    Afterword 123
    Acknowledgements 125

1

REBOOTING DUQUESNE FOOTBALL:
HOW THE CLUB PROGRAM WAS KICKED OFF

WHEN YOU LOOK BACK at the most rewarding things that have taken place in your life, it's interesting to note how many of them happened organically. You didn't really plan them. Situations arose and began to evolve. You sensed something meaningful could unfold. You recognized an opportunity, you and others dedicated yourselves to the cause, and what transpired turned out to be beyond anything you could have imagined. Well, that's exactly what happened to me – a kid from Blawnox, PA, who had just turned 20 years old. Yes, I graduated from Fox Chapel High School, but my sophistication level (on a scale of 1-10) was about zip. So, when I left home to enter Duquesne University, I carried one duffel bag. I was wide-eyed but not bushy-tailed!

My involvement with the Duquesne University Club Football Program in 1969 and the early 1970s was one of those meaningful evolutions of my life. To provide you the ending – upfront — football returned to the Bluff in 1969 after a 19-year hiatus. The team won the national championship four years later, and it remains incredibly gratifying to have played a role. Oh, and my tail did get bushy but many years later.

After more than 50 years, I still feel enormous pride to have been part of a group of students, mostly from the 13th floor of St. Martin's Hall, who launched the Duquesne Club Football Program. Some University historians might recall that the 1940-41 Duquesne Basketball Team was named the "Iron Dukes," so I affectionately named our new Club Team the "Gridiron Dukes." I played with the team in those early days, and, as Coach Dan McCann would say to me with more than a little frustration, "Sam, if only your feet could respond as quickly as I know you want them to! Big Guy, we need to get some of that passion into those feet!"

As a young athlete, I didn't choose to play football. I kind of got pushed into it. You see, as a young kid, my time after school every day was spent playing what was known as "sandlot" or "pickup" baseball. I loved baseball, and would spend hours under my covers, when I was supposed to be asleep, listening to Bob Prince's play-by-play of the Pittsburgh Pirates on my transistor radio. I gave football very little thought beyond knowing it was a game although I was aware that other kids my age were already playing on organized teams. The area of Blawnox where I lived didn't have a Catholic elementary school when I was growing up and the Catholic schools had the football teams. So that meant no organized, elementary-school football exposure for me, but in my mind who needed it, when I had baseball. There was one guy in the neighborhood who was an exception with regard to knowing something about football without the advantage of being on a team. He was Eddie Skalski. One day, when our gang was hanging out, Eddie came out of his front door holding a football. I remember asking him, "What are we gonna do with that?" This would have been about 1957-58. He confidently said that he could teach us all how to play the game. As I recall that day now, what I learned was very similar to a rugby scrum and not at all football-like. I remember thinking, "Geez, if I want to play another game besides baseball, I'd choose throwing up a basketball into a peach basket with the guys. Heck with the game of football! What was the fun in everyone just hugging each other!"

When I entered my freshman year at Fox Chapel High School, I was 6 feet tall and 200 pounds. I might not have been sophisticated, but I knew baseball. With a good dose of confidence heading in, I planned to be on the school's baseball team. It just so happened that my Civics teacher was one of the football coaches, and he approached me with, "I want you to go out for football." I very assuredly responded, "No, sir, I'm going out for baseball." But his immediate retort was, "Forget baseball. Come down to the locker room today. I want to get you a uniform." So, I'm thinking to myself that I depend on this man for my grades. I'd better haul myself down to the locker room after school today. Baseball can wait until spring.

The next thing I knew, I had a helmet and equipment for this game that I really didn't understand. But, what I did know was that there was no way on God's green earth that my mother was going to sign the obligatory permission slip that was required for me to play with the team. What I didn't realize was that my father, a man as tough as nails, got wind of the permission slip for the football team and decided it would "toughen me up" and, you guessed it, he signed the permission slip! So, I very reluctantly sidled onto the field after class the very next day for football practice – a sport I knew little about with regard to rules, positioning, strategy, speed, skill – you name it. And, I knew I was up against many kids who had been a part of organized football in elementary and middle school. Again with the sophistication...

I was assigned a defensive-tackle position – a spot that I could handle pretty well without knowing the full scope of the game. In fact, I ended up handling that position well enough that I was part of a freshman team that lost only one game that season. Slowly, my baseball goals began to fade as I made new friends and enjoyed the camaraderie of the football squad. When spring rolled around for baseball tryouts, I was spending after-school hours with Frank Ziemkiewicz lifting weights to strengthen our necks, arms, and legs. By the way, my good friend Frank, who also was not sophisticated, although he had played football in his elementary Catholic school, went on to earn an Engineering Degree at the University of Pittsburgh, became a priest in the Benedictine Order, has lead the Benedictine Military School in Savannah, GA, to great success for many years and whose football team has won several county and state football championships, is a Colonel in the Army Reserve under which he served in Afghanistan as a chaplain, and is a member of a number of Boards of Directors. How smart was I to attach myself to a guy like this! Oh, I've got to mention this: after our extremely tough workout sessions, we would reward ourselves by raiding our parents' freezers of their gallons of ice cream. I'm smacking my lips just remembering.

I went on to play high school ball all four years, but, wow, did I absolutely hate pre-season. I remember lying on the field doing stretches and feeling as if my insides were cooking and in those days being able to drink water was a reward, not a necessity! I also recall trying to dream up ways we could sufficiently stuff the keyhole to the equipment room door with chewing gum so that the coaches wouldn't be able to get out the very heat-inducing pads and helmets. But hot and thirsty or not, my love for and knowledge of football increased exponentially with each year. As I once had done with baseball, I began to live the game by studying the plays and beginning to understand the rules, strategy, and positioning.

How lucky am I that the cherished friendships I built from that team continue to be a part of my life today.

After my senior season in high school, my football coach said, "I think I can help you get some money at Edinboro (to play football)." But I wasn't interested in Edinboro. I was more of a hometown kid and looking at the local schools. During the admissions process at the University of Pittsburgh, their representative informed me that he could arrange for me to have room and board if I went out for Pitt's football team, and, if I made the team, I might be able to get a full ride down the line – music to my ears. As an aside, at that time, Pitt was not having much success on the football field – something like 1-9 the previous season. Knowing I would be playing on the line and feeling rather pumped from relative success at Fox Chapel High School, I entered Pitt's weight room that day to take a look around (remember I had been lifting with Frank). What I saw was that all the linemen who were there were at least 6'4" and 250 pounds! I had been working as a laborer on a construction crew during school breaks and in the summer, so I remained 6', but I had dropped to 190 pounds. I began thinking that, not only would I be cannon fodder among guys this huge but also, since guys this big were experiencing losing seasons, there was no way I would consciously choose to walk into daily pummeling sessions that might easily lead to unconsciousness! I retreated relatively quickly. I shifted my focus to Duquesne University, where two of my cousins were co-eds. Another plus for looking at Duquesne University was that Barry and Garry Nelson — good friends of mine from Blawnox and in my class at Fox Chapel High School (1967 graduates) — were offered and accepted basketball scholarships to Duquesne. I thought, "If they're going to Duquesne, maybe I will too." My grades were good. I was Vice President of Student Council, a lead in the class play, a trusted school monitor, and a starter on the football team. Fortunately, my credentials were sufficient to be accepted at Duquesne University.

My dormitory situation in my freshman year was interesting. There weren't enough dorm rooms on campus for all of us, so a large group of freshmen had been assigned to live at The Sherwyn Hotel, which was being taken over by Point Park College as a dormitory, but we spent as much time on campus as possible outside of classes. Some of this time, obviously, involved football – intramural, two-hand *touch* football, that is. You have to imagine that this group included a large number of former high school football players out to prove just how good they were. Considering each guy's need to exert his individual prowess in about 40 games that were being played a week, one player usually ended up in the emergency room. I can recall one particular game in which the guys from Point Park were playing the Sheiks Social Club. We would play on any city field that was available: Moore Field, Herschel Field, and others. And these games always drew large crowds. For this Sheiks game, the guy playing opposite me came off the line on one play and charged me with a forearm with such force that he knocked me off my feet very unexpectedly. Ah, my bruised ego. I began to think "heck with this!" So on the next play, not only did I mow my line guy down, but I also got to the quarterback with an equally substantial forearm. Down he went, and he stayed down. This quarterback happened to have the reputation of being one of the best in the intramural league, and there were what seemed to me to be a hoard of girls on the sideline crying about this guy being down. Of course, all play stopped, and, as I gathered in the huddle with my back to the Sheiks, our Captain Tom Manly said, "Turn around, Sam, there are about 60 Sheiks and 300 of their supporters coming toward us – all 8 of us – if we have to run, you're the slowest one of us on the team. (Another aside: the Sheiks' quarterback was fine with no need for the emergency room that day.)

The intramural league continued into my sophomore year, but it was still way too vicious. We all knew that and also that we needed to be protected by equipment and pads, because too many kids from the league were getting injured. But no intramural team was going to be the first to call "let's hit more gently!" Yeah, that didn't happen. There were a lot of guys capable of playing at a higher level. That turned out to be fortuitous for us in the not-too-distant future.

I was just starting my sophomore year in September of 1968 when a friend of mine, Paul Molini, who at that time was President of Student Government at Duquesne, offered me the opportunity to be on the university's Athletic Committee. Every committee at Duquesne had two students on it, and in this instance, he was one, and he wanted me to be the other. I was honored to be asked.

In addition to two students, the committee also consisted of two alumni — Bill Weitzel and Jim Eckenrode — and two professors — Al Raizman and Dan DeFelice — with a University Vice President in charge. We were fortunate that Father James McNamara, Vice President of Student Life, was the Chair of the Athletic Committee then.

In February 1969, five months after joining the Athletic Committee, it just so happened that a gentleman by the name of Frank Trunzo, a Duquesne Law School alum, approached Father McNamara with the idea of establishing a Club Football Program. In turn, Father McNamara soon laid out Frank's proposal to the Athletic Committee. The group voted unanimously and enthusiastically to start the program. Father McNamara, who reported directly to Father (Henry) McAnulty, the President of the University, looked at Paul Molini and said, "It's unanimous. It's going to be student-run and non-scholarship. Who do you think should be in charge?" I literally had to sit on my hand to keep from raising it as high as I could when Paul looked at me and said, "Sam, how about if you do it?" And I responded, while trying very hard to not sound like Bill Murray calling out to his sorry band of men on graduation day in the movie *Stripes*, "You can count on me!"

Back then, many club football teams were student-run, with some having an affiliation with their universities while others did not. A few were run by their Athletic Departments. It was decided that Duquesne's Club Football Team would be student-run, with a connection to the Athletic Committee, because we served on that committee.

At that time, I was living on the 13th floor of St. Martin's Hall with my roommate Ken "Curse" Curcio. I threw it out to him that we were about to start a Club Football Program. He didn't sit on his hands, but he raised both of them and said, "I'm in. What would you need me to do?" At that point I didn't exactly have an answer for him, but we both were aware that we were going to need a good bit of help. We immediately started talking to the other guys on the 13th floor — including Lou Grenci, Bob Grochowski, John "Skitch" Henderson, Gary McHenry, Bob Skoff, and others. (Another aside: these guys who volunteered their time in the Club Football Program's effort all became heavy hitters in life. Ken Curcio became the Chief Financial Officer for the Pittsburgh Pirates for a number of years until I lured him away to be the Chief Financial Officer of The Academy Schools; Lou Grenci, rose to the role of Assistant District Manager with the Social Security Administration in Ohio; Bob Grochowski, became Partner in charge of Taxation at a regional accounting firm in Baltimore for 40 years; John "Skitch" Henderson served as our team's trainer and went on to be an Orthopedic Surgeon; Gary McHenry, became the Owner/District Manager of a Lawn Care Franchise; Dave Sirhal became a Pharmacist and owned his own pharmacy in Exton, PA; and Bob Skoff, proudly served as The Dial Corporation's Executive Vice President of Human Resources for many years. All very successful careers – all a part of the foundation of Duquesne's Club Football Team. How lucky we were!)

As Curse recalls, "There was this group of guys, all members of the 13th floor of St. Martin's Hall. Everybody was willing to do whatever was necessary. That's what made it fun. It created a bond between a lot of us, which I think was there anyway, but this made it tighter. We were all focused on the same goal, which was making this football team work."

I started making a list of things we had to do. Schedule games. Buy insurance. Get equipment. All of that. Frank Trunzo, who was an attorney with PPG, was incredibly helpful with these tasks. He made a binder for us that included sections about scheduling, purchasing, acquiring insurance, and so on. He had everything documented in that handbook and advised, "Use this, make notations, and keep it current as things progress."

Bob Skoff framed Frank's influence well when he said, "Frank gave us a lot of great counsel and guidance. He was really good at making sure we weren't going off the rails in any way. If we were doing something problematic, he would rein us back in. He was super helpful."

Obviously, hiring the head coach would be a critical decision. We decided to call Pete Dimperio, the great Westinghouse High School coach (1946-1966) who became known as one of the greatest high school football coaches of all time. My mother graduated from Westinghouse and sang his praises, and my cousin started at tailback for Pete during Dimperio's coaching years there. Combining all these facts, I felt confident that we would receive top-notch counsel from Pete.

SAM COSTANZO

July 20, 1970

Dear Sam:

Hearty congratulations on your forthcoming Club Football Program! It indicates an expenditure of much time and energy and I take this occasion to thank you in the name of the Administration for this meaningful contribution to student life. I hope it will attract alumni and friends as well.

Best in wishes and prayers for a great season.

Sincerely,

Henry J. McAnulty, C.S.Sp.
President

Mr. Samuel A. Costanzo, Director
Duquesne University Football Club
201 West Saint Ann's
Pittsburgh, Pennsylvania 15219

July 27, 1970
At the request of Sam Costanzo a copy was sent to:
Mr. Burrell Cohen
Executive Director
Three Rivers Management Corporation
400 Stadium Circle
Pgh., Pa. 15212

I located Pete Dimperio's telephone number, called him, and gave him the background as to why I was calling. Simply put, we were starting a Club Football Program at Duquesne University and were looking for his assistance in finding and hiring a coach. He agreed to meet with me and another guy by the name of Pete Kulyk who came to Duquesne to play basketball.

Pete Dimperio, who was retired, lived on Graham Boulevard in Blackridge in a really nice home. When we got there, he opened up our meeting with, "Boys, I want to take you down to my humility room. That's where we'll meet." We entered a spacious room on the lower level with walls that were adorned with his many plaques and awards — including 17 City League Championships at Westinghouse High School, multiple Coach of the Year awards, and recognition of just some of his 230 players who went on to receive college athletic scholarships. His tenure at Westinghouse included a remarkable 123 wins, 5 losses and 2 ties.

It was all there on display, and it was incredibly impressive.

That day, Coach Dimperio was very welcoming and spent a great deal of time with us discussing the project. When we concluded, he suggested that we come back to see him again in a week. Kulyk and I were very happy to agree to speak with Coach once again to seek additional advice and direction – there was so much to learn! But what we didn't know at the time was that, during that week between our visits, Pete Dimperio was considering coaching our new team himself! In the end, however, Coach Dimperio decided to remain retired. He actually said to us, "Who do you think you'd like to hire as coach?"

When we told him that we were going to run an ad in the newspaper, he said, "There's a guy who played for me (at Westinghouse) who coaches at Bethel Park (High School) that you ought to consider." Of course, Kulyk and I immediately big-eyed and raised eyebrows up and down at each other – a 1969 version of a fist bump and hand explosion today. Moving on, Coach was referring to Joe Nicoletti. And, although we interviewed a few other candidates, largely based on Pete Dimperio's recommendation, we hired Joe as Head Coach of our newly formed Club Football Program at Duquesne University.

With a record of 59-27-4 in 10 seasons at Bethel Park, Joe had a proven track record as a successful coach. Thankfully, he also recommended Frank Lucido, one of his assistants at Bethel Park and a Slippery Rock alum, to be his Assistant for our football program. Our 13th floor group interviewed Frank and agreed to hire him. Frank Lucido would coach the line, and Joe Nicoletti would coach the skill position players – each of them coaching on both sides of the ball. We were rolling now!

Simultaneous to our efforts to hire top-notch coaches, recruiting players for that first season clearly was a priority and entirely student driven. It was a group effort from the 13th Floor of St. Martin's Club Football Administration relying on a grass-roots approach. Remember, there was a lot of talent and excess energy in our intramural league. In fact, the Playboys had a quarterback, Rich Carlberg, who tried out for the Green Bay Packers, got cut, and then came back, and played for the Playboys once again. He also had a successful career playing collegiate basketball for Duquesne – a very talented guy, indeed.

At the time, the intramural football program at Duquesne was led by a couple of powerhouse teams – mainly the Playboys and the Sheiks. Back then, if you played against the Playboys or the Sheiks, your team could count on getting beat 35-0, because those two teams were that good. Our team, the 13th floor of St. Martin's, usually got crushed by those guys, but we managed to hold our own against other dorm teams. So, it was among these groups that our recruiting efforts began.

Bill "Bubba" Reid was a Playboy. He played basketball for Red Manning (at Duquesne) but had since left the team and decided to come over and play football with us. Can you imagine a 6'7", 310-pound tackle in those days? That was Bubba. Jack Daurora and Gerry Buffo came out too. They were phenomenal athletes who played linebacker and guard respectively. There were several other Playboys who joined us as well — including Mickey Byrnes, John Grunick and Armond Creo. Among the Sheiks who joined the program were Eros Siano, who was a tremendous quarterback for us for two years, and Pete Rondinaro, who played multiple positions both ways. Also joining the team were William Buchko, Chuck Spezzano, John Kowalski and Jim Vumbaco.

The interest from the fraternities was not as high, but we did get a few noteworthy players from them — including Bill Casile — who went on to become a professor at Duquesne and remains a friend to this day — and also Carmen Bianco, Chuck Fenton and J.D. Roda.

2

ALL HANDS ON DECK

LOOKING BACK more than 50 years later, the task of getting the Duquesne Club Football Program up and running in 1969 was an enormous challenge. We certainly weren't armed with a big budget, and, as a student-run organization, our 13th floor St. Martin's group of friends-turned-administrators shouldered all the responsibility. But, at the same time, I can't help but feel tremendous pride about what we accomplished as kids.

It was a ton of work that required dedicating an extraordinary number of hours to the cause, and we often stretched ourselves very thinly. But you know what? We loved what we were doing, and we were doing it together. That's what made it so rewarding. (Another aside: Remember my dad wanted to "toughen me up" and signed that permission slip for me to play football at Fox Chapel High School? Well, well, well – he was not at all thrilled by how much time I was spending on football at Duquesne. In fact, in conjunction with my founding the Club Football Program, I was required to earn my own tuition also! No more help from Dad. Can you imagine that discussion with an Italian accent?!)

Pete Kulyk came to Duquesne University with a full-ride basketball scholarship, and led his freshman team in scoring. But his sophomore and junior seasons were marred by knee and ankle injuries which led to him stepping away from the team. Pete, who lived on St. Martin's second floor with other basketball players and some members of the Tamburitzans dance ensemble, was very receptive when I asked him to be the Director of the Gridiron Dukes that first year. He said, "If you love doing what you do, whatever it is — it doesn't matter if it's athletics or your job or whatever — if you love it, you don't care about spending 10 hours a day doing it. Because that's your thing. That's what you love. It was a major challenge reviving the program. There were a lot of naysayers. A lot of people said, 'Naw, that's not going to work. Club football? What the heck is that? That's no good.' But we persisted." Graduating from Duquesne in 1970 with a degree in Accounting, Pete was not only successful as a CPA but also, after rehabbing his knees and ankles, played 9 years of professional basketball in France and one year in Stockholm. What a guy!

Striving to bring order, respectability and success to our new program was very difficult for the coaches also. Soon Head Coach Joe Nicoletti instituted spring practice for our team — a very good idea that our 13th floor group hadn't thought of. Coach Nicoletti wanted to get an early look at his troops. At the same time, it gave the players a chance to get to know one another and begin the team-building process.

There were many talented players who came out for football that first year, but some guys dropped off mainly due to jobs they had to work to pay for tuition. And I personally understood that. Players would come and go, which necessarily made it difficult to practice and to make the team cohesive. That was particularly irksome to Coach Nicoletti, who was an old-school disciplinarian. He probably wanted to cut guys who didn't come to practice every day, but he was enough of a realist to understand that he needed as many bodies as he could in order to compete with the difficult 6-game schedule we had beginning in the fall of 1969. Assistant Coach Frank Lucido was a younger gentleman who related to the players a little bit better. He believed in discipline too but appreciated the fact that our athletes weren't on scholarship and had to find a way to pay for their educations — plus go to class, study, and play football. I certainly could sympathize.

Handling the logistics for the Club Football Team was considered strictly a 13th floor venture (of which Pete Kulyk had become an honorary member). Our whole floor was involved in one way or another. When we'd come back to the floor after practice and, whatever needed to be accomplished with regard to our new program, it got done. We regularly were completing Club Football tasks until 9 or 10 o'clock at night, sometimes later, and we just fit our studies and homework in when we could.

"It was a lot of work. Sometimes I remember getting back to my dorm room at like 12:30 or 1 o'clock in the morning after working on things with Sam Costanzo or Frank Trunzo or Pete Dimperio or somebody. But it was a pleasure as much as it was hard work," said Kulyk.

My roommate, Curse, was a great example of a 13th floor St. Martin's guy jumping in and helping wherever and whenever he was needed — without hesitation. And I have to say, Ken is still like that today.

"When we were getting everything going, we started to think, 'What do we need?'" Curse said. "Well, we needed a statistician. That fell on me and Lou Grenci. But Sam got me involved in just about everything. There were games where I held the chains. There were games when I went and greeted the opposing team and showed them how to get to South Stadium. I ran errands for things that the coaches needed. There were times that I would drive players to away games if they had to stay behind for a test and couldn't take the bus. We all did everything we could to help.

"In those early days, Sam used to say, 'You know, a lot of people think we're playing tag out there. That we don't have equipment, and we don't tackle. But this is real football. It just happens to be student-run.' And it was a chore, but we did it."

Looking back with perspective, it's important to keep that era in context. The late 1960s and early 1970s was a volatile time in our country with the Vietnam War going on. Like Bob Skoff said, "Duquesne wasn't Berkeley, so we were a little bit immune from all the craziness and protests that were going on at campuses around the country. But still, it was a turbulent time. So, I remember that it felt good doing something productive and constructive at a time when a lot of kids were very anti-establishment. Maybe not consciously, but subconsciously, our group wanted to do something worthwhile and valuable.

"I can't even remember who the first game was against. But I can remember thinking, 'I can't believe we actually got a team on the field,'" Bob Skoff said with a laugh. "We couldn't believe we did it. But it wasn't just that game. We still had other games too. We had to travel. We had to get buses and hotel rooms. There was still a lot to do. But looking back on it, it was like, 'Wow! We did it.'"

Those comments by Bob reminded me of something that happened prior to the 1970 season. It was then that I told Father McAnulty I had a contract with Three Rivers Stadium for two games that year and two games the next year. He said, "That's good, Sam. How much will that cost?" It was $1,500 a game, which might sound like peanuts to play at a professional stadium, but it was an enormous amount of money for us.

Upon hearing that, Father leaned forward and said, "Sam, do you know what's happening at other universities." I responded, "What do you mean, Father?" He said, "People are marching and protesting, and kids are getting hurt. You're building something up, so I'm with you 100%. Do what you need to do. Just come in and talk to me occasionally."

Talk about "The Wind Beneath My Wings," after hearing Father McAnulty's support for our efforts to play at Three Rivers, I not only thought I was flying out of his office but I also knew that we were going to make it.

Duquesne University Football Club
Samuel A. Costanzo   Director
201 West Saint Ann's
Pittsburgh, Pa.   15219
July 8, 1970

Father McAnulty
Duquesne University
Administration Building
Pittsburgh, Pa.   15219

Dear Father McAnulty:

Recently we signed a contract which will enable the Club to play its' last two home games at the new Three Rivers Stadium. Hopefully the improved surroundings will mean increased support from the community.

We have already received a great deal of support from faculty, alumni, students, administrators, the Athletic Committee, Student Congress, and various other campus organizations for which we are grateful. We are anxious to hear your views on our program. Thank you for your time.

Sincerely yours,

Samuel A. Costanzo
Director

SAC:cmb

3

ROBBING PETER TO PAY PAUL

WHILE KEN CURCIO AND I began recruiting fellow students to help launch the Duquesne Club Football Program in 1969, Curse did something that would prove to be extremely beneficial not only for our club but also for my entire life.

"I brought in a good friend of mine, Bob Grochowski, who was an accounting major with me," Curcio said. "I thought Bob would be the best person to handle the finances, more so than me even, because he was a better student than I was. I had a feel for it, but he was really good. Once I got Bob involved, Sam really took a liking to him because he was such a good numbers guy. We really entrusted that to him." Grochowski also became another honorary member of St. Martin's 13th Floor.

"Yeah, I was an unofficial member though," Bob shared. "I was a commuter, but I met Ken Curcio during the first semester of my freshman year and sort of got adopted in. I ended up spending the night there semi-regularly. I spent so much time at the dorms, people thought I was a resident. Then as far as becoming the treasurer, Sam talked to Ken about doing it, but Ken said, 'No. You should talk to Bob. He's the one making high honor roll every quarter, I'm not.' So that was how he got me in."

On the topic of how the Club Football Program was able to stay afloat on a shoestring budget, Grochowski mentioned getting some equipment donated from local high school programs, leasing other equipment, financial contributions from Duquesne alumni, and my relationship with university officials.

"Quite frankly, we sort of juggled, robbing Peter to pay Paul those first two years," Bob revealed. "The alumni came through with some money, and then Sam went to the Athletic Committee one time when we were really desperate. But it wasn't enough that we ever felt like we were comfortable."

There was a point where keeping the team solvent was beginning to seem like an impossible task to Grochowski, despite how gifted he was with numbers. In fact, he considered stepping aside — or at least threatened to do so.

Bob came to me and insisted, "You've run up all these bills, and I've got to tell you, unless you get a check for me today, I'm done!" Bob and I had become friends by this time. So, I calmly said to him, "Bob, you've got to relax." We had $5,000 from the alumni, spearheaded by Jim O'Day, who was not only a Vice President of Pittsburgh National Bank but also he had played for the last Duquesne football team in 1950! We also had $5,000 committed by the President of Student Government Rita Ferko Joyce. I knew we had the $10,000 — but it wasn't in our account —and Grochowski was upset right then. The money was in university accounts, and it had been committed to us, but it was still all university money.

So, I went to visit Duquesne University President, Father Henry McAnulty to rectify the situation and ease Grochowski's mind. I told Father McAnulty, "Father, my Treasurer is going to quit. He's going to become a CPA, and he thinks this (overseeing our Club Football Team's finances) is going to hurt his reputation." Father

Mac took a minute to consider what I was telling him and looked up and said, "Sam, who do you have money from?" And I responded, "I have $5,000 from the student government and $5,000 from the alumni."

Father McAnulty turned and picked up his telephone and called Father Duchene, who was the University Treasurer with a reputation for being very tight-fisted with money. Of course, Father Duchene was tasked with being very careful with money because that was his obligation. I heard Father Mac say to Father Duchene, "I've got Sam Costanzo here. I want you to cut him a check. How much do you need, Sam?" And I think my voice was squeaking when I said, "I'd like to have half, please."

Father Mac told Father Duchene, "Cut him a check for $5,000 and bring it over to my office right now." Father Duchene apparently was not thrilled by this request, but he wrote me a check on the spot and presented himself shortly. Again, with the "wind beneath my wings," I came back and gave the $5,000 to Bob Grochowski with a big smile and said, "Will this do?" I can remember the look on his face to this day. "I can't believe this. I'll never doubt you again. You're a freakin' miracle worker, Sam," Bob exclaimed.

When Grochowski was asked to frame other ways he was able to navigate the challenges of covering expenses, he said technology — or more precisely, the lack thereof — was a factor. "Oh, it was very stressful. It was a struggle," he said. "I kept a lot of spreadsheets. I'm glad we weren't in the age of Zoom and FaceTime. Vendors the Club Football Program owed called my house, and that was before caller ID, so I never picked up the phone. Plus, I wasn't home very much anyway.

"I was always trying to figure out who to pay. Like we had to pay for equipment because guys needed shoulder pads or hip pads. And we absolutely had to pay our liability insurance. There was a lot of schmoozing on my part, trying to get people to extend us credit, which was really difficult in those first couple years, because we hadn't made a name for ourselves yet."

Bob Skoff, another one of the Club Football Team's organizers from 13th Floor of St. Martin's, attended Churchill High School with Grochowski, and knew him well. "Bob was really good at keeping us on track with our budgets," Skoff said. "Even though he was only a year older than I was, it felt as if he were an adult and the rest of us were a bunch of stupid 18- and 19-year-old kids."

Yeah, quite simply, Bob Grochowski was a phenomenal Treasurer.

4

SPREADING THE WORD BEYOND CAMPUS IN THOSE EARLY DAYS

AS WITH EVERY NEW ENDEAVOR, positive information needs to be spread – in our case for Administration's support, for alumni support, for campus-wide student support, and for civic and corporate support. So, my next assignment was publicity. And my sophistication level by this time had risen — from zilch to an enormous two!

Was it my allure that got me in front of a television camera so quickly, you might wonder? That would be a resounding "No!" It had more to do with necessity and invention. The Club Football Team simply needed exposure, so I went to see Clair Brown, who at that time was Duquesne's Athletic Director. However, his previous position with the University had been Assistant to the Sports Information Director. In those days I was only too willing to pick anyone's brain who was able to assist in our endeavors for the team, and in this case Clair not only had contacts but he also had telephone numbers that he was willing to share. And he generously gave me the okay to use his name when I made those contacts.

As a result of those efforts, I soon found myself on television at a media interview outside of the University's Student Union building introducing our Club Football Program. I still remember the nerves I felt that day. I was about to be interviewed by both Ed Conway and Red Donnelly of Channels 4 and 11. Big stuff! I also recall, prior to the start of the Press Conference, the particular kindness that Red Donnelly showed me when he pulled me aside to tell me that he would be giving me the first question and to show me upfront what that question would be as I exhaled the deep breath I had been holding.

What I didn't know at the time was that my Aunt Theresa, the matriarch of the Costanzo family who led a group of seven family members through Ellis Island from Italy years earlier, saw that original broadcast. At its conclusion she immediately phoned my father, her brother, and told him that he had to catch the news broadcast later. Both my Dad and Mom did watch the rebroadcast of the Press Conference later that night, and the next time Aunt Theresa spoke with my Dad, she asked him with enormous pride in her voice, "How did it feel to see your name on television?" You see, I was named after my Dad, and our name was printed on the screen as I was speaking that day. My Dad may not have completely appreciated how I was using either tuition money or my time on Club Football, but football pride was beginning to seep in.

Not long after that televised News Conference, when I was in class (clearly thinking about football), I received a message that Father McAnulty wanted to see me in his office. Simultaneously with our initiating our Club Football Team's effort, the University was attempting to raise funds for the school. Well, it seemed as if news of our public relations efforts had spread among some big-city corporations, and they frankly weren't happy. Unfortunately, their first response was to jump to the conclusion that our Club Football Team was going to cost millions of dollars in addition to a fundraising effort Father Mac was invested in to fill the then-troubled coffers of the University. Telephone calls were coming in with comments such as: "How dare you spend that kind of money trying to start a football program while asking us for funds to save the college?!"

Once I was in Father McAnulty's office, he explained to me that he was getting his ear chewed off by some corporate executives' accusing him of spending millions on MY new team in the midst Duquesne's fundraising effort for greatly needed revenue. So, he said to me, "Sam, here is a list of all of the people within the city who are unhappy with me and the university right now. I want you to call each and every one of them to explain how the Club Football Team evolved, YOUR involvement in it, that it is non-scholarship, and particularly that you and your team members are taking care of all your own funding." Remember the wind beneath my wings before? This exit was with a tail between my legs…

So, I placed each and every one of those telephone calls from St. Martin's Hall's wall phone selling the devil out of our new Club Football Program, and, to my surprise, I received tremendous support from these executives. And their financial endorsements to Fr. McAnulty and the university would come front and center in a very exciting way down the road once these supporters understood that our Club Football Program was non-scholarship and that our entire budget was about $12,000 for the year.

5

READY OR NOT:
GRIDIRON DUKES HIT THE FIELD IN 1969

DUQUESNE UNIVERSITY had not played a football game in 19 years before the 1969 campaign got underway with a September 27 contest against Niagara University in Buffalo, NY.

In the days leading up to that game, Gridiron Dukes' Head Coach Joe Nicoletti reported that he had 37 players available, and Club Director Pete Kulyk told the Pittsburgh Press, "It may sound a little corny, but the guys are playing simply because they love the game and hope to eventually see Duquesne get back to big-time football."

The game ended with the Gridiron Dukes losing to Niagara, 20-0. But the score was only 6-0 late in the game despite the fact that the DU offense was hampered when halfback Tom Manly and fullback John Grunick left the game with injuries in the first half. Grunick had already gained 62 yards. "Those were two losses we could have done without. The team just didn't seem the same without them," Nicoletti told the Duquesne DUKE after the game.

With the score at 6-0, the mistakes came in quick succession — a high snap from center from punt formation and a fumble on a kick-off return — gave Niagara the ball deep in Duquesne territory. Both of those gifts to Niagara were converted into touchdowns. Coach Nicoletti indicated, "Our boys played a tremendous game on defense, but we just made too many offensive mistakes. We had 6 fumbles and 10 penalties, and you simply cannot win games playing like that." While Coach may have been really proud of the defense, at the end of that same third quarter, about 45 minutes into the game, I looked over at Bill Casile, who also played with me at Fox Chapel and remarked, "I'm exhausted." With sweat dripping down his face, Bill replied, "No kidding, Sam. If we were back in high school, the game would have been over by now." You may already know this but high school games are 48 minutes long while college games are 60 minutes long – almost a quarter longer.

The next game resulted in a rousing victory of 33-0 over St. Francis (PA) at South Stadium. The Duquesne defense played well again — intercepting three passes, recovering a fumble, and blanking the Frankies. With Grunick and fellow running back Chuck Spezzano out, linebacker Pete Rondinaro jumped in to play fullback, scoring 3 touchdowns on runs of 12 and 14 yards and a 3-yard pass from quarterback Eros Siano. Our quarterback tossed three scoring passes on the day. The others went to Armond Creo for 22 yards and Tom Piech from 3 yards out. A fumble recovery by Jim Vumbaco on the St. Francis 18 set up the first Rondinaro score, and linebacker Jack Daurora intercepted a pass and returned it to the Frankies' 27, which led to the Piech touchdown.

(A painful aside: The win was definitely an exciting one. But I had broken my left hand in the Niagara game which called for me to wear a plastic cast over it. For Piech's three-yard run our team was lined up with yours truly playing guard. The ball was snapped, and I opened the hole and drove my man to the goal line where we both hit the ground. Their linebacker advanced to meet our running back and, in so doing, stepped on my hand and broke the plastic cast. Yes, I did stay on the ground for a minute or two, but there was not a bunch of girls crying on the sidelines for me!)

After the contest, Nicoletti told the Duquesne DUKE, "We were really lucky in that we were getting good field position. Against Niagara, we were always starting out in the hole, but in this game we kept getting good field position, and that helps." Regarding the heroic performance by Rondinaro, Coach said, "We had to go with Rondinaro (at fullback), and we just asked him to do his best. His three touchdowns tell an impressive story."

The Duquesne basketball team enjoyed a terrific 1968-69 season, going 21-5 under Coach Red Manning and participating in the NCAA Tournament. But I remember something funny that happened when the Club Football Team beat St. Francis for our first victory in 1969.

That is that some young women hung a sheet on the tunnel heading to Duquesne's men's locker rooms that said — We *love you Gridiron Dukes*. Later, in the cafeteria, there were fans lined up, and everyone was hugging us.

After I took my tray back to the kitchen area, I decided to join my long-time friends Barry and Garry Nelson at the basketball team's table, and Barry said to me: "We're supposed to be one of the best teams in the country in Division I basketball. You morons go out there and win one Club Football game, and every girl on this campus is cheering for you guys." Bubba (Reid), who had been a basketball player but was playing football with us, chimed in with, "But, Barry, either you've got it or you don't."

After St. Francis, Duquesne had two weeks to prepare for Fordham, which was ranked No. 1 in the country at 3-0 and had not allowed a point in those three games. Prior to the matchup, Daurora said, "I'm going in expecting to be hit, and hit hard, but ready to hit 'em right back." It wasn't a surprise that he would feel that way — because Daurora was one tough guy.

"He was a monster at linebacker," Ken Curcio remembers. "I think that guy could have played at a higher level. He was memorable. He was very physical, and he liked being physical. He had a Jack Lambert kind of style."

And Bubba Reid, the Gridiron Dukes' 6'7", 300-pound lineman, said, "Sure, Fordham was tough, and we respected them. But we didn't expect to lose like that." The final score, however, turned out to be Fordham 36, Duquesne 0. All 5 touchdowns by the visitors came via the run including a pair by 220-pound fullback, All American Eric Dadd in the fourth quarter. By the time Dadd scored his two TDs, the Gridiron Dukes were worn out.

The score was 15-0 at halftime. Passes by Siano to Spezzano (33 yards) and Ron Connelly (18 yards), who was our tight end and also played for the Dukes basketball team, had the ball on the Fordham 2-yard line with 1 second remaining in the half. However, Siano — who completed 15 of 30 passes on the day — was stopped short of the goal line on a keeper on the final play of the half.

Despite the defeat and the lopsided score, Duquesne also had earned respect. Fordham Coach Jim Lansing was quoted in the Duquesne DUKE saying, "It might have been a little different in the second half if they would have scored then (right before the half). Duquesne has a tremendous team for a first-year club. Their defense is really good. They really crack out there."

"We have 15 good men filling 22 positions, which means a lot of guys have to go both ways," Coach Nicoletti reported after the game. "The players were really beat in the second half. We ran out of gas."

After a narrow 14-12 loss to St. Vincent, Federal City was next on Duquesne's schedule. Although the Panthers were also a first-year program, they arrived in Pittsburgh at 5-0, ranked No.

4 in the country, averaging 44.6 points and 450 yards of offense per game.

And they manhandled Duquesne, 60-0, at South Stadium.

I almost scored my first touchdown that day. I had been playing offense in the Bonaventure game. Coach Nicoletti was becoming frustrated that their quarterback kept completing button-hook passes to his tight end. He finally yelled out, "Can anybody stop that play?" I proudly said, "I can!" Nicoletti instructed, "Then get in there and do it!" Well, the very next time the Bonnies were in a third down and long situation, where we knew they would pass, I was ready. As the quarterback dropped back, I stealthily slid into the hook zone, staying low, and at the last second, I popped up in front of their tight end. The quarterback, looking for the tight end, threw the ball, and it hit me in a bad place, right in my hands, and I...dropped it! No touchdown. No glory. Was I razzed! "Nice catch, Sam."

With the victory, Duquesne closed its first season back on the football field with a 2-4 mark. "This was put together pretty quickly to have a team in 1969 that had to take the field," Curcio said. "You know, we were 2-4, but I thought for a first-year team we were very competitive."

1969 DUQUESNE UNIVERSITY GRIDIRON DUKES ROSTER

NO.	NAME	POS.	HT.	WT.	CLASS
10	Eros Siano	QB	5-10	160	Jr.
11	Carmen Bianco	HB	5-4	170	Sr.
12	Mickey Byrnes	QB	5-11	175	Soph.
20	Tom Manly	HB	5-10	175	Soph.
21	Pete Rondinaro	HB	6-0	175	Sr.
22	Jack Rodgers	HB	6-1	170	Soph.
30	J.D. Roda	HB	5-10	165	Jr.
31	George Sikon	HB	5-8	170	Soph.
32	John Grunick	FB	6-2	225	Sr.
40	William Buchko	HB	5-10	174	Soph.
41	Armond Creo	HB	5-7	165	Sr.
42	Chuck Spezzano	FB	5-10	180	Sr.
50	Shaun Lally	C	6-0	222	Sr.
51	John Kowalski	C	5-10	200	Sr.
52	Richard Ferraro	E	6-3	220	Sr.
60	Gerald Buffo	G	6-0	200	Jr.
61	Sam Krause	E	5-11	185	Jr.
62	Rodney Dixon	HB	5-9	165	Fr.
63	Panfilio DiCenzo	LB	6-2	225	Jr.
64	Tim Galvin	G	6-2	198	Sr.
65	Sam Costanzo	LB	6-0	205	Jr.
66	Jack Daurora	G	6-0	220	Jr.
70	Steve Jennings	T	6-0	220	Soph.
71	Bill Casile	G	5-7	205	Sr.
72	Ernie Walker	T	5-8	220	Fr.
73	Chuck Seifert	T	6-1	210	Soph.

74	Harry Dudro	T	6-3	210	Jr.
75	Dave Beck	T	6-0	250	Fr.
76	Bill Reid	T	6-7	280	Sr.
80	James Vumbaco	E	6-0	170	Soph.
81	Jim Breisinger	E	6-0	175	Soph.
82	Ronald Connelly	E	6-2	190	Sr.
83	Chuck Gilch	E	6-1	180	Sr.
84	Moe Barr	E	6-4	185	Sr.
85	Bill Robinson	LB	6-2	205	Sr.

Head Coach: Joe Nicoletti
Assistant Coach: Frank Lucido
Managers: John Henderson, Joe Dumovich
Club Director: Pete Kulyk

6

COACH NICOLETTI MOVES ON

AFTER THAT FIRST SEASON, Frank Lucido, Joe Nicoletti's assistant, informed me that he was taking a new job and leaving teaching. That was a significant loss. The players loved Frank. He was a little younger, he related well to the guys, and they respected him, because they knew he had been a small college All-American at linebacker for Slippery Rock. Frank was also an excellent teacher of fundamentals, and his competitive spirit motivated all of us.

When he left, our 13th floor group had to hire someone. We had to find Joe a new assistant. We put an ad in the newspaper, and I couldn't believe the response we got for an assistant coach position. We must have gotten around 60 responses. Club ball or not, it was college football, and, if you were a high school coach, you wanted a shot at that position. Ken Curcio, Bob Grochowski, Lou Grenci, Bob Skoff, and I started interviewing prospective candidates. But first we had to narrow the list by looking at resumes. We couldn't interview 60 people.

After a thorough review of all the resumes, we interviewed approximately 10 applicants. It was then that Joe came to us with the name of a guy he felt should replace Lucido. "I need a line coach, and this is the guy for the job," he said. We were happy to interview the guy, and he might have been a good line coach. I couldn't say. But it was clear to us that he wasn't going to relate well to the players. Joe was a good guy, a good coach, but he was very strict, and that is where we saw his choice of a line coach leaning also. We were looking for the same balance that Coach Lucido lent. Joe's candidate did not do well in our rankings.

Frank Trunzo, the attorney who had been assisting us, knew of our dilemma and came to us with the suggestion of a coach by the name of Dan McCann. Our group interviewed Dan and ranked him among the 10 candidates. Dan had an incredible run of success as the freshman coach at North Catholic High School. Another prospect, Charlie Scales, played for the Cleveland Browns, the Pittsburgh Steelers, and the Atlanta Falcons — a running back for seven years in the NFL (1960-1966) – was interested in coaching the Club Football Team. Pretty exciting stuff for us! So, we put Charlie through the interview process and ranked him also.

We proceeded through the entire process, finished the 10 interviews, and the 13th Floor Club Administrative Group ranked all the candidates to determine our top two picks. The decision was that we would go with either Dan McCann or Charlie Scales for Assistant Coach. I telephoned Joe Nicoletti and asked to meet with him about the new coach position.

Shortly after that call, Nicoletti and I went to a restaurant in Oakland, Frankie Gustine's, to discuss the situation over dinner. Joe said, "Well, what did you think?" I was very up front with him, "Joe, I've got to be honest with you, we're not going to hire your guy. We've got a couple of really good candidates, and we'll give you the option of picking from those two, but our favorite is Dan McCann."

With a furrowed brow Joe replied, "You're going about this the wrong way, Sam. My guy is the man for the job. What has McCann done?" I told him without reservation, "Dan went 27-0 with his freshman team at North Catholic." I said, "Frankly, Joe. I don't care if you're coaching kindergarten. I don't mean to be disrespectful, but undefeated is undefeated, and 27-0 is very impressive."

The discussion continued on in the same vein – back and forth. But, ultimately, I repeated to Joe, "We're not going to hire your guy, and, to be completely honest with you, of everybody we interviewed, our group had him finishing dead last."

As a result of my position, Joe Nicoletti felt so strongly about his candidate *not* getting the job that he decided to step down at that dinner meeting as Head Coach of the Gridiron Dukes. That definitely was not the outcome we were seeking. Our student group will always be grateful for the many contributions Joe made in getting us through that first year. The 1969 team had to overcome many obstacles, and our 13th floor group of student administrators knew we owed Coaches Nicoletti and Lucido a debt of gratitude for assisting us in that endeavor. We now faced another hurdle.

I went back to campus and told Curse what happened. We felt confident that we had a couple of good men and coaches in Dan McCann and Charlie Scales. Our consensus was that we would go with McCann as Head Coach and Scales as Assistant Coach.

That's how it ended with Coach Joe Nicoletti, and a new era under Coach Dan McCann.

As it turned out, Charlie was only with our program one season — 1970 — sending the 13th Floor of St. Martin's Club Administrative Team back to a coach search. As luck would have it, Dan brought in Jim "Pro" Vrbanic for us to interview, and every member of the Administrators gave "Pro" a huge thumbs up. He turned out to be one hell of a coach, and, with Dan and "Pro" as the coaches, our team really took off.

7

McCANN TAKES THE REINS & ROD HESS'S CATCH

SHORTLY AFTER THE FALL SEMESTER began in 1970, an article was printed in Duquesne's student newspaper carrying the headline "Grid Iron Dukes Return for Their Second Season," and in the article it mistakenly spelled the last name of Duquesne's new Head Football Coach as Dan "McKann" in more than one spot. However, it didn't take long for Dan *McCann* to become a household name.

Dan had coached Catholic grade school football in the Pittsburgh area at St. Joseph's in Manchester and at St. Sebastian's in the North Hills (a quick note: Dan's team played against other squads that were being coached by Dan Rooney, the son of Pittsburgh Steelers, Art Rooney Sr., and Tom Foerster, the future Chairman of the Allegheny County Commissioners) before moving on to North Catholic High School where he went undefeated in three seasons as coach of the freshman team. His cumulative record prior to accepting the Duquesne position was said to be 69-4-1 over 10 years. What's more, McCann — whose "real" job was serving as Vice President of Sales for the Pittsburgh Brewing Company — was outgoing, energetic, and personable. And he had an incredibly sharp football mind.

"I was in on the interviews for the new coach, and Dan stood out," Ken Curcio said. "He just lit up the room with his enthusiasm and his 'let's-get-it-done' attitude. I don't know that we'd be where we are today (in 2024) if it hadn't been for the way Dan got the program started. He was a very good coach and a tremendous motivator."

Prior to the 1970 season opener, McCann told Dan Donovan of the Pittsburgh Press, "We're going to work hard at being successful. I've been a winner all my life, and I'm not going to stop now."

Approximately 20 lettermen — among them quarterback Eros Siano, halfback Tom Manly and linebackers Jack Daurora and Gerry Buffo — returned from the first-year Club squad that went 2-4 in 1969. The schedule for Season Two was expanded to eight games with four home games — two would be played at South Stadium and two at Three Rivers Stadium, the new home of the Pirates and Steelers. Three Rivers had just opened in July that year, and you can imagine how excited the Gridiron Dukes were to be playing there.

Initially, I was able to negotiate a deal with Three Rivers Management Corporation that would allow us to play a pair of games at the multi-purpose stadium in 1970 and two more in 1971 - for, you might remember, $1,500 a game. With Western Pennsylvania being a hotbed for football, I didn't want people to think Duquesne's Club Football Program was like a beer league. Rather, I wanted everyone to realize it was true intercollegiate football. My thinking was that, if we had the opportunity to play some of our games at Three Rivers Stadium, just maybe our team would garner some respect and prestige.

While Dan McCann would go on to serve as Head Coach at Duquesne University for 19 years (1970-1983 and 1988-1992), his very first game at the collegiate level was a 41-6 rout of the College of Steubenville on the road. The Gridiron Dukes scored the first 3 times they had the ball that day and built a 28-0 lead by halftime.

The scoring began on DU's second play from scrimmage when Rod Hess hauled in a 60-yard pass on a halfback option from Mickey Byrnes. For both the second and third touchdowns, Byrnes scored on runs of 22 and 5 yards respectively.

Steubenville, playing its first game as a club program, didn't get on the scoreboard until the fourth quarter. Duquesne ran up a 335-148 advantage in total yards for the game, and 246 of those yards were on the ground. J.D. Roda had 70 yards and a TD on 10 carries, and Bob Mongillo picked up 82 yards and a TD on 8 attempts. Rod Hess, in his first game as a Gridiron Duke, closed out the scoring with his second TD catch of the day by snaring a short pass from reserve quarterback Mike Altrudo near the Steubenville 20-yard line and by breaking several tackles on his way to the end zone.

Even though the Gridiron Dukes were a second-year program on a tight budget, we flew to the Windy City for the October 3 contest with Loyola. The match-up came about at the behest of Duquesne University Dean of Students Harry McCloskey whose relative worked for Loyola.

Dean McCloskey called me into his office one day and asked how the 1970 schedule was shaping up. I told him that our schedule was almost full, and he quietly said while smoking his cigarette, "How would you like to play Loyola of Chicago?" What I didn't know that day was that he had already made a bet on the game with his relative for a few bucks or maybe a case of beer. And, while a Chicago trip certainly sounded exciting for our team, I felt I had no choice but to say, "Dean, I really appreciate it. But we're already scheduled to play Fordham this season. That's going to be an expensive trip. I not only have to pay to bus us to New York City but I also have to pay for the hotel and meals for the team and coaches. Our budget won't be able to handle another long-distance trip." His calm counter to that was: "Sam, if you play Loyola of Chicago, you can fly, and you can stay two nights in a hotel. I'll pay for it." With a Cheshire-cat grin on my face, I replied, "We're in! We'll play them!"

So, the very next week the Gridiron Dukes were on an airplane for Chicago. Keep in mind that in those days flying was not done as frequently as it is today. What I'm trying to convey here is that many of our guys had never, ever flown before – including me. But I was trying to be reassuring to those team members who were looking a bit green/gray, and my method of reassurance took on the face of a clown. Up and down the aisles I went trying to be an entertainer, trying to be a mood lightener.

Well, we ended up beating Loyola of Chicago, 40-12, as Mongillo scored 3 first-quarter touchdowns on short runs and had 4 TDs on the day. Meanwhile, the defense forced 3 turnovers — 2 fumble recoveries and a Gary McHenry interception. DU once again jumped out to a 28-0 lead, but Loyola scored twice before halftime to make it 28-12. Another TD by Mongillo was a 14-yard run in the fourth quarter which had him finishing the game with 129 yards on 21 carries. I never did find out what Dean McCloskey won in that bet…

Remember the Dean afforded us an additional night in the hotel? We used that extra night to party, enjoying the win into the early morning hours! Not too many hours after the celebration ended and after very little sleep, we all devoured a large and bountiful breakfast fit for a winning team. Do you remember that guy who was clowning around up and down the plane's aisles on the inbound Chicago flight? On the outbound flight back to

Pittsburgh, he was attempting to contain that breakfast he had just enjoyed as it was coming back up and into one of those small brown bags provided in each seat. And I was the only one on the plane in that condition!

(As another aside: I kept busy as the Director of Duquesne's Club Football Squad for that trip, because I had a severely sprained ankle and torn ligaments that prohibited me from playing in the Loyola game which was very disappointing. However, later it was that very injury that caused me to be classified by the Army as 1-Y at the Induction Center while many other men around me there were likely on their way to Vietnam.)

After returning from our Chicago victory, McCann's task was to prepare his players for the first home game of the season — against Niagara University at South Stadium on October 10. His message was, "You can't live in yesterday. You've won two games, but now we've got to think about Niagara." Niagara, you may recall, had blanked Duquesne, 20-0, in the 1969 season opener and also had a 2-0 record upon arriving in Pittsburgh. The Gridiron Dukes were definitely feeling some pressure.

South Stadium was a muddy, rain-soaked mess for the second meeting between the two teams, but McHenry returned the game's opening kickoff 96 yards for a touchdown. At halftime, with DU holding a 6-0 advantage, Niagara's Assistant Coach Eddie Olsewski let it be known that we were "a wholly different team" and "looked much more organized than last year."

The Golden Eagles blocked a Duquesne punt and scored a couple of plays later, on a short run, to tie the game in the second half. Niagara threatened to find the end zone several other times, but the Gridiron Dukes' defense recovered four fumbles — two by freshman nose guard Jeff Leon.

Near the end of the game, McCann put his gun-slinging mentality on display. Despite the terrible weather conditions, Duquesne went for the victory by attempting a long pass, but Siano was intercepted. In fact, it took a great tackle by Manly on the return to prevent a game-winning touchdown by the visitors. Since the Gridiron Dukes also failed to score again, the game turned out to be a hard-fought, 6-6 tie. Not bad considering the previous year's 20-0 loss...

After the team's 2-0-1 start, I was quoted in the Duquesne DUKE as saying, "I feel the interest here has doubled in the last year, and with our stronger schedule, I think it's a better program all the way around. I realize that Coach McCann is tough, but that's why we hired him. We have faith in him and his system."

In that same article, Pat O'Neil of the DUKE wrote: "The Dukes' stock is on the rise. They are gaining respect." Ah, you can't imagine the pride we were feeling, but, hold on — we lost three of our next four games — 12-0 on the road against Fordham on October 17; 41-6 at South Stadium against St. John's on October 24; and 28-2 vs. King's College at Three Rivers Stadium on November 7 – our homecoming game. And here's something to consider: According to the New York Times, Fordham, St. John's, and King's College were all nationally ranked clubs in the Top 10 in the country.

Rod Hess had an interesting story about that beating we took from St. John's on October 24. Rod recalls the story this way, "It seems the visitors didn't want to come out of the locker room, because the previous night Pittsburgh's Catholic High School League played on the South Stadium field, and, as a result, it was a sea of dried, hardened tufts of mud and divots. Coach McCann was upset with St. John's. He was trying to get them to come out, but their coach emphatically insisted, 'No, you've got to clean that field up first.' So, we waited and waited in our locker room while the maintenance people did what they could to smooth out the dried mud and plug the divots, but Dan became impatient. Then, Dan, Sam Costanzo, and I went back into St. John's locker room, and

Dan demanded, 'C'mon, let's go!' Dan turned to Sam and asked him, 'Did you give them the check?' (for the travel guarantee) Sam said that he had, so Dan sternly let St. John's coach know: 'You've been paid. Let's get this game going, or I'll claim the forfeit!' And, when the St. John's coach still refused, McCann announced, 'Aw, you guys are nothing but a bunch of chicken shits!' Well, that was all they needed to hear. It turned out that Dan was, once again, the great motivator that day. We lost 41-6." Motivation indeed…

One of four games that we did win was the first-ever college football game at Three Rivers Stadium. On October 31, Duquesne University triumphed 34-6 over St. Vincent College. In that game, Rod Hess became the first collegiate player ever to score a touchdown at the new stadium.

We were very, very excited to be playing at Three Rivers Stadium in this matchup. As it happened, the New York Jets were scheduled to play at the stadium against the Steelers the very next day. So, to my mind, we have Saturday, they have Sunday. No problem… until I received a phone call from Steelers' executive Jim Boston. Jim called me and proclaimed, "Sam, the Jets are coming in, and they need to practice." I responded, "What does that mean, sir?" Boston's strong retort was, "It means you're out of there, because I have a contract with the Jets that says they get to practice at one o'clock on Saturday." "But I have a contract that says we play at one o'clock on Saturday, Mr. Boston. So, we're playing ball," I replied. Then in even stronger tone, Boston replied, "Look Kid, we're the Steelers. The Jets are taking the field!"

Fortunately, Steelers' owner Dan Rooney was a Duquesne alum who was fond of our football program, and he urged Boston to work something out with us. So the Steelers' exec called me back suggesting, "Sam, how about this…if your team could play your game at 11:00 a.m., the Jets could take the field at 1:00 p.m. for practice." I thought that was reasonable and that we could work that timing out.

Our game was going along rather well when the Jets' Joe Namath came out to the sidelines with Don Maynard and a couple of other receivers. They began throwing the ball around while mingling among us and watching some of our game. At one point Dukes' quarterback Eros Siano threw the ball to Rod Hess, and Rod made one of the greatest catches a football fan could ever see. The ball got tipped by the defensive back, then Hess tipped it. The ball then went over Rod's head, but he caught it behind his back with one hand. Hess fell down but brought the football in for a touchdown!

Playing defense for the Gridiron Dukes that day, I also was standing on the sidelines during Rod's play when I heard Joe Namath say to Don Maynard, "Maynard, if you could catch the damn ball like that, I'd already be in the Hall of Fame." We were all awestruck in the presence of Broadway Joe, and after meeting Namath, I bought a pair of white spikes just like his.

With still no publicist to promote our Club citywide, a lunch invitation gave this kid from Blawnox his first personal experience with another celebrity by the name of Myron Cope. The Curbstone Coaches Luncheon used to be held downtown at the Pick-Roosevelt Hotel. During this second year of our Club Football Program, Penn State Coach Joe Paterno, who had been scheduled to be the main speaker, was unable to make an appearance at the last minute. So, someone put my name in the hat, and I was called with a "Can you come in and present Duquesne football?" Offered the chance, I said, "Sure, I'll be there."

The emcee of the luncheon was Myron Cope. As he approached the podium, he introduced everyone, and he then said, "This guy over here is a kid from Duquesne University. He's a junior there. What the hell is he doing here? He's supposed to be in math class.

Why aren't you in math class, Sam? You've got to learn something. You can't be down here with these bums."

When it was my turn to speak, Myron ribbed me with the same lines — the whole routine all again – can you hear Myron's famous nasal twang? Finally, I had the opportunity to talk about the Gridiron Dukes, and it was wonderful to get our program exposure with a serious football audience like that. But I was more than a bit unnerved...

When the luncheon ended, a reporter from either the Post-Gazette or the Press came over to talk to me. Still pretty nervous, he said something to me along the lines of, "You remind me of a movie star." To ease some of the tension I felt, I replied jokingly, "Boris Karloff?" He said, "No, no, no. The guy who played in that Russian movie (snapping his fingers in an effort to recall)." The newsman finally remembered the movie as *Dr. Zhivago* and then spouted out, "Yea, Omar Sharif." Again, I'm still thinking more Boris Karloff, but he finally got on with the interview about our Club Football Program.

However, the next day, I saw a story in the city-wide newspaper that read, "Bluff's Omar Runs DU Football as Club Director." Well, our guys bought what seemed like 50,000 copies and stuck them up all over campus — in the cafeteria, on the 13th floor, on other dorm floors, and on every bulletin board they could find. The comparison was a huge compliment, but I ended up taking an enormous amount of ribbing for it. In fact, "Skitch" Henderson, our trainer and future Orthopedic Surgeon, who was also a great artist, couldn't resist drawing a caricature of me as Omar Sharif and submitting it to the Duquesne DUKE where it was printed in the next issue. Show me red-faced...

The Gridiron Dukes finished the season with a 4-3-1 mark after being awarded a forfeit victory over St. Bonaventure for a game that had been scheduled to take place in Olean, NY, on November

14. Although Duquesne didn't sustain its early-season momentum and experienced a couple of tough losses along the way, there was no doubt that the Club Football Program had made progress under Dan McCann in Season Two.

"I think Club Football is good for Duquesne," Dan told the Duquesne DUKE toward the end of that 1970 campaign. "The kids are playing for the love of the game not for a scholarship like other universities. It's a genuine sacrifice for these kids. They get no reward. They love the game, and they have a great attitude."

On the other hand, looking toward the 1971 football season for the Club Football Team, Bob Skoff, who succeeded me as Director of the Gridiron Dukes, recalls Dan McCann this way, "Besides Xs and Os, Dan was really a great motivator. The players would have crawled over broken glass for the Coach. Gary "Mac" McHenry was a safety, and on one occasion during the past season, Mac's arm was black and blue from his forearm to his shoulder. I said to him, 'Mac, what are you doing out here today?' Because of McCann's dedication, motivation, and example, there was just no way that McHenry would not be going out on that field that day."

In 1937, Duquesne University was a national football power, defeating Mississippi State 13-12 in the 1937 Orange Bowl.

Francis J. Trunzo, M.D.

CLASS OF 1929

GOOD LUCK DUKES

13th FLOOR Sweetheart – LINDA FEDOREK	**Patrons**
CARMEN BIANCO ARNIE CASCIATO SAM COSTANZO KEN CURCIO JOE DEMOTT JOHN DOVALOVSKY HARRY DUORD JOE DUMBOVICH GARY FRYE LOU GRENCI BOB GROCHOWSKI JOHN HENDERSON JOHN KAUFMAN BOB McCOLL GARY McHENRY JOHN NEIDERER, Jr. BILL RYAN MIKE SHAUGHNESSY BOB SKOFF JOHN STONEK CRAIG STOTT BOB TOMMASONE BILL TRUSHEL RUSS ZANDONELLA	JOE MADIA BARBER SHOP FRANK TRUNZO TAU DELTA TAU MARK LEVIN BROTHERHOOD JAMES KIRK COLONEL WIGHT JOHN CURLEY RICHARD PACKARD PARAPHERNALIA CASHIER'S OFFICE EMPLOYEES DR. GLICK M.N. ZEOLLA OLD ALLEGHENY DUCHY
SAYS **Go Gridiron Dukes**	

COMPLIMENTS OF

"A Friend"

BEST OF LUCK FOR NEXT YEAR

[10]

St. Martin's Hall 13th floor Duquesne Club Football Administration.

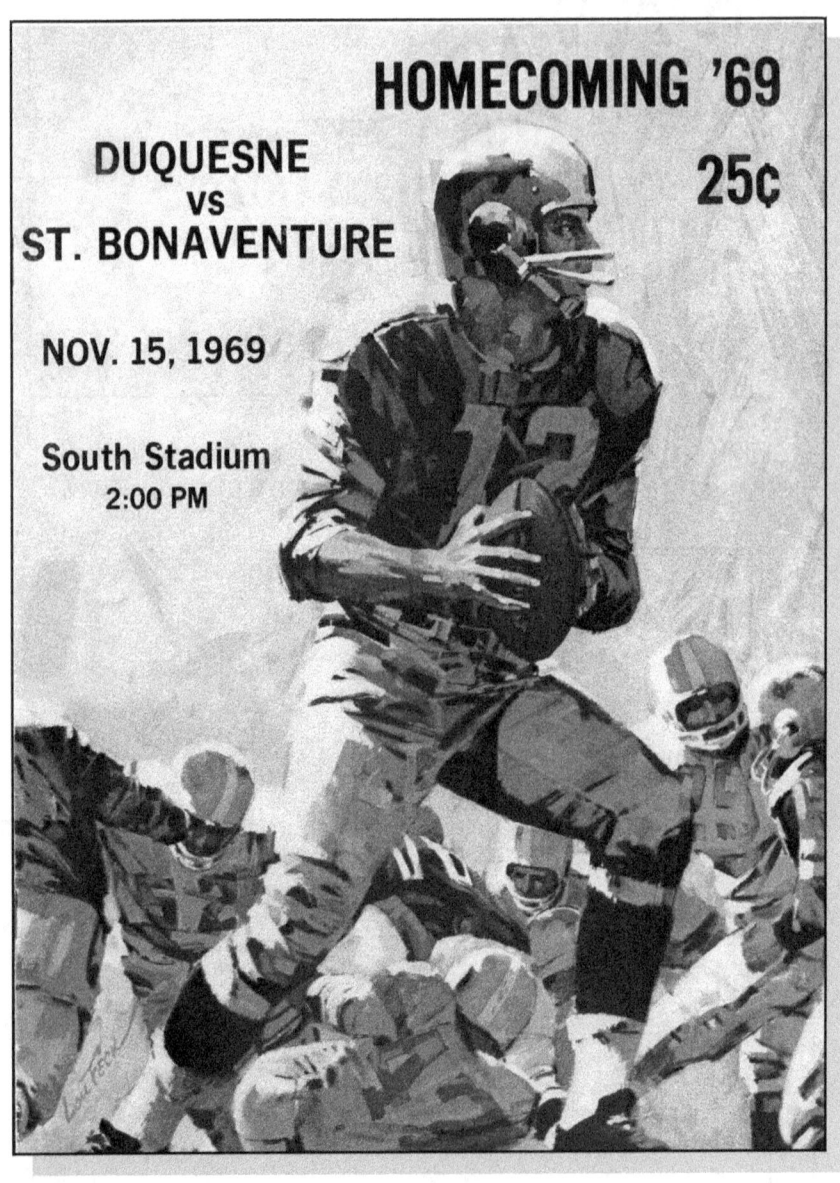

Game program cover, first Club Football Homecoming.

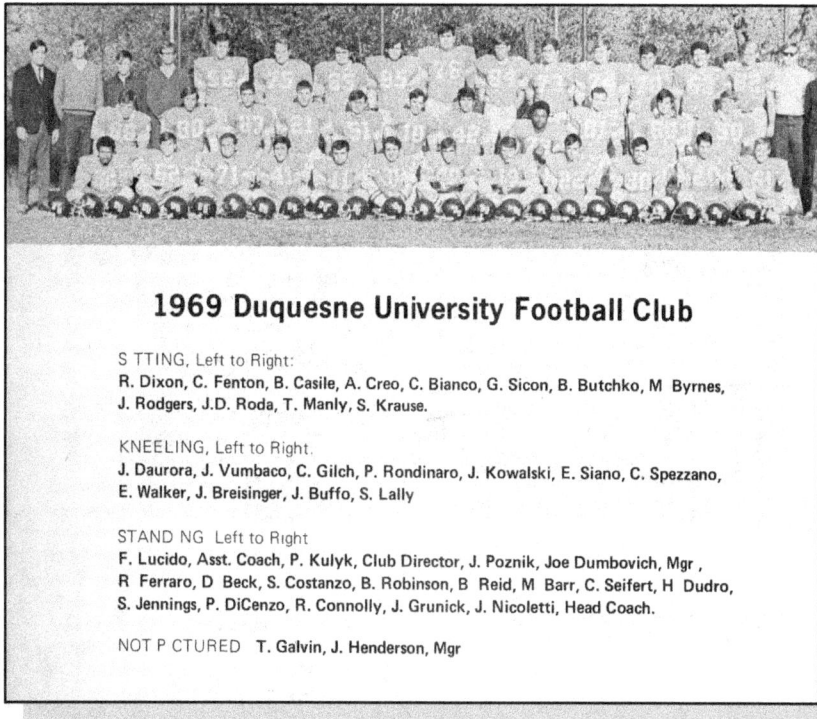

1969 Duquesne University Club Football Team

CLUB FOOTBALL
1971 Budget

PLANNED INCOME

522-02	Student Congress	$ 14,000
	Alumni Association*	7,500
	Guarantees (4)	5,350
	Gate Receipts	2,000
594-00	Athletic Department*	1,500
	Amount Requested	TOTAL - $ 30,350

EXPENDITURES

522-18	Rental Three Rivers Stadium - 2,000 rent - 3,000 expense	$ 5,000
	Debt Reduction	3,000
522-18	Coaching Staff - 1,200 Head Coach - 800 Asst. Coach - 500 Asst. Coach	2,500
	Guarantees* - 350 St. Francis - 350 Steubenville - 1,500 Catholic University - 1,500 Chicago Loyola	3,700
522-18-256	Travel Away	5,150
522-18-441	Equipment Lease*	2,500
522-18-704	Insurance	2,000
522-18	Home Game Expense	1,700
522-18-101	Supplies	2,000
522-18	Medical Deductible (insurance)	750
522-18	Pre Season Expense	1,000
522-18	Other Miscellaneous Expense	200
		TOTAL - $ 29,500

* Fixed costs - Reduction not possible

1971 Club Football season budget

Head Coach Dan McCann poses against Duquesne University athletics timeline inside the Cooper Fieldhouse.

Head Coach Dan McCann calls a play on the sideline.

Gary "Mac" McHenry turns the corner as All American tackle Jerry Kresge leads the way vs. Niagara in 1972

Grid Iron Dukes team leaders with coaches Dan McCann and Jim Verbanik: John Stefanik, Jack Schroeffel, Steve Sherer and Rod Hess.

Halfback Steve Sherer breaks tackle for a touchdown at Three Rivers Stadium.

Wide receiver Rod Hess scores against St. Vincent.

Front page of The Duquesne Duke, November 24, 1973.

1973 Duquesne University National Club Football Champions

Grid Iron Dukes featured a Top 10 Club Football offense.

Head Coach Dan McCann with his Grid Iron Dukes 2021 reunion.

8

CLUB FOOTBALL IS NO JOKE

FROM THE APRIL 16, 1971 EDITION OF THE DUQUESNE DUKE STUDENT NEWSPAPER

"WE CHALLENGE YOU MR. PAGLIA"

Duquesne Duke Sports Editor's Note: Last week Tony Paglia of our staff wrote an article called "To Fill A Void" in which he pointed out that one major sport on campus isn't enough. Something must be done to fill the gap. He went on to say that football should go big time. Its present state leaves something to be desired. The following is a rebuttal from the Club's National President, Sam Costanzo and Director, Robert Skoff.

Dear Mr. Paglia,

While browsing through the April 2 issue of the DUKE, we came across your brilliant article "To Fill A Void." We are so glad to see all the encouragement you are giving ambitious students striving to improve their school. For a campus that has moved from almost total apathy to a great deal of involvement, you certainly are a shot in the arm.

Here is one of your caustic quotes: "When the pigskin sport is blooming all over the country, it is almost a joke at Duquesne." Try telling the kids who have worked for two years to bring football back to the Bluff that it is a joke. Maybe it was a joke to all the people who attended games, or to the Pittsburgh sportswriters who wrote us up each week whether we were home or away. Our alumni donated $10,000 to our program in the last two years; maybe they think it's a joke too.

You go on to say, "If it (club football at Duquesne University) is to be a future of small ideas and goals, then why go on?" Perhaps you have never bothered to discover the goals of club football's aims are to enable college men to play legitimate contact football at a low cost, without causing the University three-quarters of a million dollars in expenditures. The men that play club football are not stars across the nation, but they are guys who love the game and are willing to play without scholarship money. They play for the game itself with the hope that it will unite the school in the fall as basketball does in the winter. The 3,000 people who attended the homecoming game this fall (2,000 of which were students) proved that club football is on the way towards accomplishing this "small goal."

Some of the other "small goals" we have accomplished are: In two years we went from intramural tab football to intercollegiate hard-hit football. We went from South Stadium to Three Rivers Stadium.

Incidentally, Duquesne University is the only club team in the nation to play in a pro stadium. For your information, there are 80 clubs around the nation and the idea is catching on fast. Robert Morris, Point Park, (Allegheny) Community College, and Pitt-Johnstown have all expressed interest in the program. Carnegie-Mellon is considering moving to a club set-up since it's the only equivalent situation. Duquesne club football has moved from a small struggling program to a club that held a district delegate post last year. This year we hold the national presidency and will compile the national rankings.

I almost neglected to comment on your ingenious ideas about big-time football. Maybe you should consider the facts. Big-time football runs between $500,000 and $1,000,000 per year to operate. Besides, the perennial winners like Notre Dame, Alabama and Ohio State are all losing money, unless they are lucky enough to make a postseason bowl. The cost of recruiting, traveling, scholarships and coaches' salaries is unbelievable. I challenge you, Mr. Paglia, to go to Father McAnulty's office and suggest spending $500,000 so you can schedule Pitt and Notre Dame.

We would like to thank Terry Coyne and Dave Hildebrand for the excellent coverage football received this fall in the DUKE. Of course, they were interested in printing the facts and giving a deserving program some encouragement. To the fellows who you also put down, Mr. Paglia, that are trying to get club hockey and soccer going, we say. "Give 'em hell, and don't let one sportswriter discourage you. If you are serious and you give it everything you've got, no one will think you're a joke."

The next time you need to "Fill A Void" Tony, just print your picture.

Sincerely,

Samuel A. Costanzo *Robert M. Skoff*
President of the National *Director of the Duquesne*
Club Football Association *University Football Club*

9

FOOTBALL SEASON 1971
A SEESAW YEAR

THE 1971 FOOTBALL SEASON began with a great deal of hope for the Gridiron Dukes' squad. You know the old trop "Do you want the good news or the bad news first?" Well, I'm going to start off this chapter with some neutral news.

Although my father continued not to be entirely on board with the time I spent growing in my favorite sport, by 1971 I had risen to be National President of Club Football. From the beginning of Duquesne's involvement, league-wide game statistics had been compiled, analyzed, and rank-ordered by Ken "Curse" Curcio and Lou Grenci. So, I had a good bit of faith, strength, and confidence behind me, as National Club President, when I reported the College Club Football information to the New York Times each week. Among the data I was responsible for and turned over was cumulative win/loss records, team ranking as it shuffled each week, and the overall subjective/non-subjective commentary on specific players, plays, and teams throughout the league. Everybody was an expert... And, as the National Club President

I was also responsible for arriving at a consensus, in the best way possible (remember there was no Zoom then) – after multiple telephone calls on the old coin-operated, wall telephone – with as many of the 80 nationwide Club Directors as possible regarding who would be named All-American for that year. My name had been proposed for All-American for the season (I think someone wanted to borrow my car), but I withdrew it, of course, not only because there were Gridiron Dukes who were better football players than I was but also because it was simply the right thing to do. This experience from the inception of the Club Football Program through to the President of the National Club Football Association set me on a path in life for which I will always be grateful. That experience afforded me strength, confidence, cooperation, humility, generosity, kindness, and more. How lucky was I...

Now for the good news...despite the challenge of what was being referred to as "one of the toughest Club Football schedules in the country," there was optimism that the Gridiron Dukes would take another step forward in 1971 — the program's third year overall and its second year under Dan McCann.

1971 saw 15 lettermen return from the squad that went 4-3-1. Chief among them were players such as second-team All-American receiver Rod Hess, productive and reliable running back Bob Mongillo, and standout defensive back Gary McHenry.

Eros Siano, a two-year starter at quarterback, graduated in 1970, so finding a replacement at that key position was a priority and would be a tall order given the leadership and talent he brought to the team. Another goal expressed by Coach McCann was having more bodies on hand — a deeper roster so fewer guys needed to play on both offense and defense.

The '71 schedule definitely presented some challenges. While we were slated to play all four home games at Three Rivers Stadium that year, the road schedule was daunting. Three of the four road games were against St. John's, King's College and Niagara, all nationally ranked teams that Duquesne had gone 0-2-1 against at home in 1970. But we continued to have some believers…

A season preview article that appeared in the Duquesne DUKE concluded with: *"In only its third year, club football is making great strides on the Bluff. Another winning season, and some more fans at Three Rivers Stadium, could lengthen those strides considerably."*

The September 25 season opener against the College of Steubenville displayed a dominant performance by the Gridiron Dukes, who won 47-6. Rod Hess caught 3 touchdown passes (of 15, 44, and 43 yards) from 2 different quarterbacks – 2 passes from Jack Schroeffel (including 1 on a Statue-of-Liberty play) and 1 pass from Mike Altrudo.

Schroeffel, who transferred to Duquesne from Drexel University, proved that he was up to the task of taking over behind center by completing 10 of 17 passes for 164 yards and 3 touchdowns. Meanwhile, the Duquesne defense intercepted Steubenville quarterback Tom Busold 4 times, 1 of which Rod Dixon deftly returned 70 yards for a touchdown.

Afterward, McCann told the Duquesne DUKE, "I think we were in much better condition physically than the Steubenville team. They seemed worn out in the second half while our kids were still going strong. Our five weeks of practice really paid off especially that tough week that we had at South Park before school started."

When asked what he liked about Dan McCann, Rod Hess told the student newspaper, "Let's put it this way, the man knows his football. He knows what he's doing every second on that field. His enthusiasm has really worn off on the team, and, hopefully, it will wear off on the student body too."

Unfortunately, the positivity of the resounding victory over Steubenville didn't last long, because one of the Gridiron Dukes — Ed Goodwin, a junior lineman from the Syracuse, NY, area — was badly injured in the game. The front page of the October 1, 1971, edition of the Duquesne DUKE included a picture of Ed's being carried off the Three Rivers Stadium turf on a stretcher.

The diagnosis was a gut punch none of us expected. Ed Goodwin had suffered a broken neck while making a tackle on a screen pass in the third quarter. After initially being rushed to Divine Providence Hospital from the game, Goodwin underwent surgery at Mercy Hospital that night. His parents, Mr. and Mrs. Dwight Goodwin, came to Pittsburgh and stayed in St. Ann's Hall on the Duquesne campus while their son was hospitalized. Each day the campus chapel was filled with students' solemnly praying for Ed's recovery.

But then the unthinkable happened…

Goodwin, a 20-year-old, third-year pharmacy student, died from complications due to that injury on October 4, 1971, just 10 days after the Steubenville game. A week after that, a memorial service was held in his honor in the ballroom of Duquesne University's Student Union Building.

"We had the whole campus there for the memorial service. It was an extremely sad time losing a teammate and a classmate like that," said Bob Skoff, who served as the Director of the DU Club Football Team that year. "Ed Goodwin was just a regular guy. Just a good-hearted guy who wouldn't hurt a fly. It was just a freak accident. I can remember vividly going over to Mercy Hospital and visiting him. It was devastating."

Just two days prior to Ed's death, the Gridiron Dukes had registered their second straight victory by defeating St. Francis, 41-13, at Three Rivers Stadium. Duquesne built a 34-0 halftime lead with the help of a pair of touchdowns from Tom Nameth (1 receiving and 1 rushing) and another long interception return for a touchdown by Rod Dixon.

However, following the tragic loss of our teammate, we all began questioning whether or not the next game, which was away at St. John's, should be played. In fact, some members of the media even called for the team to be disbanded. "I really thought the program might not survive," Skoff said. "Just one of the reasons was that there was a column either in the Press or the Post-Gazette that was very critical of us, saying we were doing things on a shoestring budget which meant that we weren't being safe and that we had no business being out there. Since we were really playing for the love of the game and nothing else, that criticism really stung."

"There were people saying that we should disband Club Football, that guys shouldn't die playing," Hess said. "People were asking what we were going to do. Were we going to cancel the season? Were we going to go on? Then Ed's parents let us know, 'No, don't cancel the season. Eddy would want you to play.'" Once Coach McCann, Bob Skoff, and I had a chance to absorb what Eddy's parents conveyed, we called a meeting with the football team in the Duquesne Room on campus to discuss among all of us what our future should be. We came out of that meeting with the decision to push forward with the season.

Rod continued, "Despite the support of his parents, though, some guys didn't want to play in the St. John's game out of respect for Eddy, and some guys dressed but wouldn't play. This tragedy kind of tore us apart a little bit, so we definitely struggled after Ed's death. We played some tough teams and ended up at 4-4 for the season. It was tough." After all, what kid doesn't think he's immortal? What kid even thinks about dying in a game that they love playing? After all, we're just playing…

Tough indeed. Though the Dukes went on to play the remainder of their eight-game schedule, things did not go well for the team.

Duquesne dropped a 35-12 decision to St. John's and then lost 3 of its next 4 contests to fall to 3-4 for the year. Coach McCann's squad finished at the .500 mark only because the season finale was a forfeit win over Catholic University.

"Between the tragedy of Ed's death and the serious financial issues that the team and the university were having, I don't know how we got through that season to be honest," Skoff said.

10

GRIDIRON DUKES TAKE GIANT STEP FORWARD IN 1972
& STEVE SHERER JOINS THE TEAM

THE REBIRTH OF DUQUESNE FOOTBALL certainly didn't result in immediate success. Satisfying victories and tough losses were experienced in equal doses during the program's first 3 years as the Gridiron Dukes compiled a 10-11-1 mark. Nonetheless, the march toward respectability had already been in progress when the team flexed its muscles — game in and game out — in 1972 — Dan McCann's third year as Head Coach. That season, Duquesne's Club Football Program finished third in the Nation's Club Football ranks with a 7-1 mark. Let me tell you how that evolved...

The 1972 campaign was running back Steve Sherer's first with the Gridiron Dukes, and he became a star. After playing at Central Catholic and later Bishop Boyle during his high school days, he spent a season at Appalachian State where he was the starting tailback on the freshman squad. However, Sherer returned to Pittsburgh the following summer. "I loved the football at Appalachian State. It was really good football," he shared. "But I found out that my mother had cancer, and I really didn't want to be 800 miles away. I felt like I should be closer to home."

According to John Stefanik, the first day he arrived along with some of his fellow cronies — namely, "Stevie (Sherer), Timmy (Kelly), Terry (Russell), and me, Dan McCann called a meeting for us to get our equipment, but we didn't know him from Adam. It wasn't like he recruited us or knew us. And we were a little bit older.

"Coach asked, 'Who did you guys play for?' I told him we played in high school and then for a sandlot team, the East End Warriors. McCann replied, 'Oh, that's rinky-dink football. You must be rinky-dink football players.'" To be continued…

At the urging of Rod Hess (who played with Steve at Central) and John Stefanik (who played with Steve at Boyle), Sherer enrolled at Duquesne and joined the football team. A preseason injury to Bob Mongillo (a crushed vertebra in his neck) created an opportunity for Sherer to take on a substantial workload. He wound up rushing for 817 yards and scoring 13 touchdowns (11 on the ground, 1 receiving, and another on a punt return). What an exciting player!

In 1972, Duquesne threw the ball well too. Quarterback Jack Schroeffel passed for 1,155 yards and 11 TDs with Hess's 39 catches, 529 yards, 4 touchdowns and freshman Sammy DeMarco's 17 catches, 248 yards, 2 touchdowns as his favorite targets. "Jack was as good as any quarterback I saw while I was at Appalachian State," Sherer said.

"McCann loved to pass, and that's what we relied on Dan's first couple of years, the passing game," Hess shared. "But with the addition of Stevie Sherer, who became a two-time All-American at Duquesne, the running game took off. So, it all kind of came together in '72."

The passing attack was on display during a satisfying 26-16 season-opening victory over Niagara as Schroeffel threw for 263 yards and tossed TD passes to Hess, Jack Horgan, and Gary "Mac" McHenry. The triumph avenged an 11-5 loss at Niagara the previous fall when the Gridiron Dukes believed the officials were far too influential in the outcome. And remember the battering of 20-0 we sustained from Niagara in our first season in 1969. We were moving on now!

Next Duquesne pounded Allegheny Community College, 29-0, as the defense surrendered only 77 yards total to ACC. The Gridiron Dukes put 3 touchdowns on the board in the second quarter as Schroeffel ran for 2 scores and completed a 26-yard pass to Terry Russell for the other. An interception by Bob Rusak and a George Sikon's fumble recovery set up those first 2 scores. Terry Russell proudly recalled, Dan had us throwing the ball more than anyone else threw the ball, and he wasn't afraid of that. Dan would always say, 'The quickest way to get into the end zone is to throw the ball over everybody's head.' And we had receivers like Sammy DeMarco, Rod Hess, and me. We could do it. We could get down field pretty quickly."

Duquesne added only 7 points after halftime, but the fact that Coach McCann pulled many of his regulars in the fourth quarter was a factor. "We could have beaten them by more if we wanted to," Dan said after the game. "But there are a lot of dedicated boys on this team, boys who never miss a practice, and I wanted to give them some playing time."

Then came a match up with King's College, which had beaten Duquesne the previous two years. Sherer particularly remembers the scene at a muddy Stone Field in North Park for the 1972 contest. "We were coming out on to the field, and King's had something like 55 guys, a lot more than we had." he said. "They looked like Notre Dame out there with uniforms like ND's – shiny gold helmets, gold pants, and white jerseys. Jerry Kresge was a team leader, and I remember he turned to me saying, 'Steve, everything's going to be okay. We're going to take these guys.' And we did. We just had a field day running the football."

Sherer actually had his Duquesne coming-out party that day — rushing for 230 yards. He opened the scoring in the first quarter with a 73-yard TD dash. Then, with the score tied, 6-6, King's returned the second-half kick-off for an apparent touchdown, but the play was wiped out because of a clipping penalty. DU went up 14-6 in the third quarter when Schroeffel connected with Mike Altrudo on an 8-yard TD pass and hit Hess for the 2-point conversion.

In the final quarter, the Gridiron Dukes fumbled deep in their own territory to set up a 2-yard TD run by Terry Jones of King's, but their 2-point conversion failed, and DU still led, 14-12. Kresge tackled King's quarterback Bob Krehley in the end zone for a safety on the final play of the game. The Gridiron Dukes registered a hard fought 16-12 victory over King's to improve to 3-0 on the season.

"We were just running off tackle the whole game. Straight power running," Sherer said after the victory. "Our line did a great job blocking — especially Jerry Kresge and Mike Aul. I'm not the kind of runner who breaks tackles. Our line was just tremendous." I happen to disagree with Steve's assessment of himself by the way. He was brilliant at setting up his blocks, and his quick and precise cuts left defenders in the dust. And, yes, he definitely broke tackles! I guess he was so fast that he didn't even sense them…

Next was a trip to St. Francis (PA) to take on the Red Flash who were club football's top-ranked team at the time. Duquesne had beaten St. Francis handily at Three Rivers Stadium the year before, 41-13, but Coach McCann warned the team not to go into this game thinking we were going to blow out the Frankies this year.

A primary weapon for St. Francis was fullback Jay Roberts, but Duquesne was able to neutralize him. "They thought they could break Roberts loose against us, but our defense bottled him up every time he got his hands on the ball," McCann said. That effort was led by the Dukes' defensive line — nicknamed the "Iron Wall." That line included John Schnitzer (end), Kresge (tackle), John Rosinski (tackle), and Rich Sprys (end). St. Francis managed only a field goal in the first quarter and a safety in the third due to our "Iron Wall." Russak thwarted a Red Flash drive in the second quarter by intercepting a pass on the DU three-yard line. Also in the second quarter Kresge returned an interception to the St. Francis 14, which led to Sherer's first touchdown with the Gridiron Dukes. In the fourth quarter, another turnover set up DU's other touchdown. Sprys intercepted a pass at the St. Francis 13, and Sherer scored from a yard out a few plays later. That year's game was a much more competitive contest from the previous year's with Steve Sherer running for 83 yards and a pair of touchdowns in a 14-5 victory.

"They had some pretty talented, big-time players, but we handled them at their field," Sherer said. "We played great defense, we moved the ball, and we beat them."

Duquesne went on to defeat Cleveland State, 12-8, to move to 5-0 on the season, with a 34-yard punt return for a touchdown by Sherer in the fourth quarter providing the winning points. After that contest, McCann said: "We've got a damn good chance to go all the way."

But it was not to be. The Gridiron Dukes lost their still-new, No. 1 ranking when they suffered a 22-20 setback at Canisius the following week. The defeat was both painful and controversial.

Duquesne held a 20-8 lead against Canisius at the end of the third quarter, but disaster struck in the fourth quarter. Stefanik, the All-American linebacker, tore ligaments in his knee and had to be helped off the field. The Golden Griffins then scored two touchdowns, and the margin of victory came on a two-point conversion with a minute and a half left in the contest. This loss deprived the Gridiron Dukes of an opportunity to play for the National Championship in the Boardwalk Bowl in Atlantic City. So close…

Compounding Stefanik's serious injury, however, Russak told a more revealing story about the Canisius contest. In an article written in the Duquesne DUKE, he reported: "We were fighting the officials, the weather, and Canisius, and we beat the team and we beat the weather, but we couldn't beat the officials."

From the same article came this:

The officials were the same ones that took care of Niagara in their 11-5 win over the Iron Dukes last year (also in Buffalo). They haven't changed much. They screened the Duquesne defensive secondary all game, and one of them even grabbed Russak by the shoulders during a play. They called a clip on a punt return, then couldn't identify the offending (DU) player. They allowed late hitting by Canisius and overlooked two occasions when a Duquesne receiver was tackled when the ball was still in the air.

Some year the Iron Dukes may have an undefeated season. They might defy all the odds and go unbeaten. But this is not the year. Their hopes for going 8-0 were shattered on Oct. 21, 1972, when on a rain-drenched field in Buffalo they lost a 22-20 decision to Canisius College.

"We got homered at Canisius and that knocked us out of the No. 1 ranking down to No. 3," Hess said. "Coach McCann said we had a shot at a bowl game — some consolation bowl — and left it up to us as to whether or not we wanted to play in that bowl. Some guys wanted to go, and there were other guys who didn't. But why play in a bowl like that? So that Canisius game was our downfall."

Hess believes the '72 team may have been even better than the '73 squad that won the National Title.

"That could very well be," Sherer said. "In that game against Canisius, we just couldn't hold on." "I think '72 was the start of something pretty good," the then-injured Stefanik offered. (An aside: Another linebacker who was relied on by the Gridiron Dukes, especially when Stefanik was out, was John Hoch, a terrific guy and an excellent football player. A few years ago, I learned from John at a Homecoming game that, once again, the Club Football Team made a difference in the future of its players. John's interest after graduation was in Marketing, and his initial pursuits began with the local department stores Horne's and Kaufmann's. However, at that time, there were no openings for him. He did learn, though, that there was an opportunity with a major department store chain in San Francisco, so Hokey flew out for an interview with high hopes. John met with the Vice President of Merchandising, Herb Friedman, but, as the interview was winding down, John did not feel the interview was a touchdown. Finally, Mr. Friedman, perusing John's resume, took note that John played Club Football for Duquesne University. Friedman asked John, "You played Club Football at Duquesne?" And John acknowledged that indeed he had. The next question out of the VP's mouth was, "Did you know Sam Costanzo?" Hoch told him, "Yes, Sam was a teammate of mine and has been involved with the team since its inception." Then Friedman asked Hokey, "What would Sam say if I picked up this phone right now and asked him about you?" John replied, "He would say I was hard-working, loyal, and that I take great pride in whatever I do." Hokey finished the story by saying that the Vice President of Merchandising declared: "You're hired!" You see, Herb Friedman had been a Club Football Director for St.

John's when I was Club Director for the Dukes, and I had collaborated with him on multiple occasions. Talk about a small world… That story made me proud once again that our program helped make another mark on one of our player's lives.)

Meanwhile, getting back to opinions as to whether or not the '72 or '73 team was better, Tommy O'Malley, who was in his first season as the Publicist for the Duquesne Club Football team in 1972, wanted us to remember, "Dan was always prepared whether it was a meeting with a bar about selling them beer or coaching a football game. He was well prepared, knowledgeable, and persistent as hell. He was all about winning, and nothing held him back." As Coach used to say in 1971, "We were starting to win, and people didn't want to play us." "The word was out. Don't play these guys. They can beat you." Stefanik recalled.

And Tommy's observation about Coach McCann was becoming increasingly apparent. But that didn't hold Dan McCann back…

11

LITTLE SAMMY FROM SOUTH CATHOLIC

I HAVE A RATHER INTERESTING STORY about one particular player who came to play with the Gridiron Dukes in the fall of 1972. That spring of 1972, a guy named Sammy DeMarco had an excellent year in baseball as a senior at South Catholic High School and had plans to play that sport for Coach Bobby Lewis at the University of Pittsburgh. However, Title IX — which was designed to eliminate inequities between male and female athletes — became law shortly after DeMarco graduated, and his Pitt opportunity fizzled.

"Baseball was my game, and that didn't work out. I was completely bummed out about it," he said.

Fortunately, Sammy DeMarco — all 5'7" and 150 pounds of him — also had excellent skills as a wide receiver in football and that opened a different door. Sammy then moved his focus toward football and Duquesne University's Club Football Program.

Both Linebacker John Stefanik, and Flanker Rod Hess, who was an All-American for Duquesne by then, remember the first day of practice in 1972. "Sammy was a little guy with a big ego," they agreed. "A bunch of us were standing around one day when Sammy approached us with, 'Hi, I'm Sammy DeMarco. I made all-conference at South Catholic.' We all just looked at him and simultaneously replied, 'So.' But, thinking back on that day, we should have given the guy credit for having the courage to approach the existing team members at all. Pound for pound he was a tough guy. He really was. Sammy was an excellent receiver, and he could definitely run." And with that DeMarco quickly became ingrained into the team.

"I was a little nervous about going to Duquesne. I was just 17. I was just a kid, he recalled. But I wasn't there 20 minutes, and I was starting already. Jack Schroeffel was the quarterback, and he spotted me right away during one of our first practice drills. So, I got called out with the first team offense at that initial practice and then for every game I remained first team.

"I was young, and I was pretty brash," he admitted. "I wanted to play, and I wasn't afraid to stick up for myself." I recall someone pointing out to Coach McCann, "This freshman, Sammy DeMarco, isn't sitting well with some of the older guys." And, as Dan McCann put his thumbs in his waistband, lifted his chest, shifted his legs akimbo and then crossed his arms, he stated in no uncertain terms, "I don't care what they think, Sammy DeMarco's going to catch a lot of footballs at Duquesne."

As a freshman in 1972, DeMarco was the Gridiron Dukes' second-leading receiver with 17 catches for 248 yards and a pair of touchdowns, behind Hess, who had 39 receptions for 529 yards and 4 TDs. "I had a good season my first year, even though the other guys were older," DeMarco said. "We had really good players on that team that finished 7-1. We just didn't have a lot of players."

"Sammy DeMarco was an unsung hero for us," reported Terry Russell, who played a variety of positions for the Gridiron Dukes and played them all well. "He didn't get enough credit. Sammy was *really* good." "When I found out that I couldn't play baseball at Pitt, it broke my heart," DeMarco said. "But as it turned out, I wouldn't trade the experience of playing football at Duquesne for anything in the world. That has stayed with me to the present day."

12

SETTING THE STAGE FOR CHAMPIONSHIP GLORY

BY 1973 the Gridiron Dukes were a dominant team that ran roughshod over the competition. They lost only a handful of players from their highly successful 1972 squad and returned four players who had earned All-America honors — receiver Rod Hess, quarterback Jack Schroeffel, running back Steve Sherer, and linebacker John Stefanik. Exciting times! But, wait, there was a fly in the ointment!

Sherer became hampered by a hamstring injury that affected his availability and production. He didn't play in the season opener vs. Allegheny Community College on September 9 or in the October 27 game vs. St. Vincent's. After rushing for an outstanding 817 yards in 8 games in 1972, Sherer gained only 386 total yards in the 1973 regular season due to his injury.

Another difficult issue was that Schroeffel was declared ineligible — a process that got underway at the urging of a rival coach from St. Francis which was considered the powerhouse in the Club

Football League. This coach happened to be a North Sider who apparently went way back with Dan McCann, and it just so happened that there was some bad blood between them. Jack Schroeffel had been a freshman at Drexel University in Philadelphia after he left North Catholic High School and played some while at Drexel. No one at Duquesne felt as if Schroeffel's participation was sufficient enough to deem him ineligible, and, frankly, we were shocked that he was ruled out for 1973. The instigator, of course, in a typical North Side move, waited until right before the season started to issue his complaint.

That move could have been devastating for Duquesne except that McCann, who recruited non-stop, had Davey Thomas — a transfer from Mississippi State and also a product of North Catholic High School — waiting in the wings. "Fortunately, Davey Thomas was on the team as a back-up quarterback and a safety. He became our quarterback, and he was a real good one," Tommy O'Malley added.

"I loved Jack Schroeffel. I started from the first game on because of him, but Davey Thomas was the real deal too," DeMarco said. "Davey could really sling it. He and I were on the sidelines throwing all the time before he became the starter. So, we already had a rapport."

"Davey was a skilled, Division I quarterback," Sherer added. "He was a little younger than Jack, and he did a really good job for us." Thomas stepped in behind center and took the team the rest of the way, completing 72 passes in 149 attempts for 1,014 yards and 9 TDs while Rod Hess led the team with 29 receptions for 464 yards and a pair of touchdowns.

Duquesne blanked its first three opponents — Allegheny Community College, Niagara, and American University — by a combined score of 74-0. Steve Sherer scored 3 touchdowns in a 34-0 romp over Niagara. In the fourth game, the Gridiron Dukes

— already ranked No. 1 in the country — surrendered their first points of the season, but it was only a field goal, in a 14-3 victory over St. Francis (PA).

Steve Sherer remembered this about Dan McCann, "Coach McCann was really good to the players. Very fair. He demanded a lot. He demanded that you be a good student, that you be a gentleman, that you be a good teammate. I'm really proud to have played for Duquesne, and I'm eternally grateful for my experience there."

The only real test of the regular season came the following week when Duquesne traveled to Wilkes-Barre, PA., to take on King's College once again. A 68-yard TD reception by Sammy DeMarco helped the Gridiron Dukes build a 14-0 first-quarter lead, but King's punched back to lead 15-14 at halftime. An 86-yard kick-off return for a touchdown then swung the momentum strongly in favor of the home team. But that didn't shake Duquesne. In the fourth-quarter Sherer ran for 1 touchdown, and DeMarco (who had 119 yards in receptions against King's) put another on the board lifting Duquesne to a 26-15 victory over King's that day.

After that win, 3 more shutouts ensued — 18-0 over Catholic University, 23-0 over Canisius, and 12-0 over St. Vincent. Toss in a forfeit victory over Steubenville, and Duquesne finished the regular season with a 9-0 mark — outscoring the opposition 167-18 and registering 6 shutouts. Remarkably, the Gridiron Dukes didn't allow a point in the second half of any of those three games nor did they surrender a rushing touchdown.

"We were third in the country the year before. We had most of our people coming back, and some younger kids coming on board, so we started to get some hype." Stefanik said. "We were thinking, 'Hey, we've got a chance here (at the National Title).'"

"When we started playing, we were shutting teams out. We had six shutouts, and St. Francis only got a field goal, so really you could throw that one in there too. Remember Niagara had previously beaten us pretty badly. Usually we scored points in the high teens or low 20s, but there were big goose eggs on the defensive side. Coach McCann was great at taking an opposing team apart by finding every weakness they had. He would say, 'Our guy is better than their guy here, here, and here. These are the plays we can run – this play, this play, and this one.' He could identify every weakness they had and say, 'This is what we're going to do against them.' And it worked – 90% of the time he was right on."

"We could play defense with anybody," tight end Terry Russell added. "We really could, because we were fast, and we just had tough, dedicated kids. That season, the defense often led the way, in part because the offense had to overcome a couple of key challenges," including Sherer's injury and Schroeffel's elimination. Rod Hess had more to reveal about Dan, "Coach McCann was always very organized and disciplined. That was his obsession. He just oozed football. He would always say, 'If I'm not here for practice, that means I died. We're going to practice no matter what!' He was very dedicated to what he was doing. He was always looking for ways to get that edge on the opponents."

After the impressive regular season, McCann worked to bring No. 2 ranked Mattatuck Community College of Connecticut to Pittsburgh for the National Championship Game at Three Rivers Stadium. He did so with help — financially and logistically — from Allegheny County Commissioner Tom Foerster, the Allegheny County Police Association, and Pittsburgh-based companies such as Gulf Oil, PPG Industries, H.J. Heinz, Westinghouse, and ALCOA. The November 20 game was billed as the Children's Hospital Bowl benefitting Children's Hospital of Pittsburgh.

13

THE MONSTERS OF MATTATUCK

TOMMY O'MALLEY recalls that Dan McCann and Jim "Pro" Vrbanic had the opportunity to fly to Connecticut to watch the Mattatuck Chiefs play their 1973 regular-season finale. The Gridiron Dukes' publicity man also remembers that our Head Coach and his Assistant were blunt when he asked them what kind of a squad was coming to Pittsburgh for the National Championship Game.

"I remember talking to them after they came back from Connecticut, and Dan cautioned, 'We're going to have a tough game on our hands, Big Guy. They're pretty good,'" O'Malley said, "Then Jim looked at me and with more than a little concern on his face revealing, 'Tommy, they're going to kick our ass. All their guys are big, and they've got like a 100 of them. They're really good.'" The "a 100 of them" part was clearly an exaggeration, but "Pro" had made his point.

Duquesne's All-American receiver Rod Hess said Vrbanic shared a quick story with him as well after the trip to scout Mattatuck. "Jim said he and Dan were on the plane coming back from Connecticut. They had all their notes in front of them, and McCann revealed, 'I'll tell you what, Big Guy, I'm sure glad I'm not playing in this game,'" Hess recalled, "But, you know what, Dan didn't tell us that story until after our game though. He just said, 'They're big, but we can beat this team.'" Always the motivator...

All-American linebacker John Stefanik said the Gridiron Dukes weren't too concerned about who would provide the opposition. They were confident in themselves and determined not to let any team stand in the way of capturing the National Title.

"Pro" was a straight shooter who used that North Side lingo when he said, 'Mattatuck is stacked, and they're big as a house,'" Stefanik remembered. "At first, I responded, 'You're kidding me, Coach.' But we didn't care. We were prepared to play anybody."

On game day, however, it became very apparent well before kick-off that the reports about Mattatuck were accurate. The visitors — who went 7-0 during the regular season and averaged nearly 30 points a game — were indeed huge. The official program for the National Championship Game listed 8 of the No. 2 ranked Chiefs at 225 pounds or more and a whopping 32 who weighed in at least 200. You know how some teams tend to exaggerate their individual team members' heights and weights on game-day programs. Let me emphasize. There was no exaggeration as to the sizes of these young men on Mattatuck's team! Meanwhile, Duquesne had just 3 players who were reported to weigh 225 pounds or more — center Mike Aul (225) and tackles Tom Makin (230) and Mickey Lebret (240) — and a total of 10 guys tipping the scales at a little over 200. And I won't reveal if we were stretching the stats...

Mattatuck, as it turns out, brought a couple of busloads of players to Pittsburgh — 65 guys to be precise — to go up against a Gridiron Dukes' squad that would dress only 32 players. "We're out on the field warming up at the far end zone. I saw a group of guys coming out from the other team in these white uniforms with black numbers, and I thought, 'What? They're our size!'" Hess said. "And then somebody told me, 'That's just their special-teams, Rod.' Soon, more players just kept coming out and coming out and getting bigger and bigger and bigger.

"We were all looking at them, and I tried to reassure not only myself but all the guys around me, 'Don't worry about it. They can only put 11 guys on the field at one time. We've got this. This is our night.' But inwardly I was thinking, 'Holy shit, we're in for a battle.'"

Publicist O'Malley was friends with four-time Super Bowl winner, Mike Wagner, who in 1973 was in his third year as the strong safety for the Steelers. The two men happened to be standing together on the sidelines when Mattatuck's squad came out onto the Three Rivers Stadium turf en masse.

"Wagner said to Tommy, 'These guys are bigger than the guys I play against,'" On this subject John Stefanik shared. "Then our players came out, and Wagner asked Tommy, 'Where's the rest of your team?' O'Malley had to tell him that *was* our whole team. But it was exciting, and we felt like we could win. We thought like the Steelers of the 1970s thought. 'Hey, you're not going to beat us. Our guys are still tougher than your guys.'"

Despite the Dukes' being ranked No. 1 going into that contest, Ken Curcio was among those who felt Duquesne would have been a decided underdog had there been a betting line on the game because of the mismatch in size and the number of players each team had available. "Just watching them come out onto the field was intimidating. It was David vs. Goliath, it really was," he said. "But we went out there, and it was really a great atmosphere," the longtime team Administrator and Statistician shared.

In retrospect, I can't help but wonder if Mattatuck hadn't also scouted out the Dukes prior to our contest with them. Imagine if they did and their scouting report was that we were a good team but small – nothing to worry about. They could dispatch us with ease. Heh…heh…heh…

14

THE NATIONAL CHAMPIONSHIP GAME
THE CHILDREN'S HOSPITAL BOWL

ANYONE WHO WITNESSED the Mattatuck Chiefs' taking the field at Three Rivers Stadium on November 20, 1973 — two days before Thanksgiving — knew why the visitors from Waterbury, CT, believed they could intimidate Duquesne's Gridiron Dukes in the National Championship Game. Never mind that Duquesne came into the game ranked No. 1 in the country with a perfect 9-0 record that included 6 shutouts.

No. 2 Mattatuck (7-0) brought many more bodies to the fight that day than the Gridiron Dukes (I'll remind you — 65 compared to the Dukes' 32), and, as it has been established, its players were much bigger than the host team's. Estimates were that the size difference amounted to 25-30 pounds a man along both lines. Seriously...

The first time Duquesne had the ball, on a running play, flanker Rod Hess took his assigned defensive back out to the right and away from the action. "As I jogged back to the huddle, their DB approached me with, 'If you catch a pass on me, I'm going to break your effin' neck,'" Hess recalled. "I just laughed and said, 'Okay.'"

With a clear size advantage, the Chiefs were confident they could control Duquesne's running game, so they were determined to unnerve Hess — just one of the Gridiron Dukes' All-Americans. And the taunts continued…

"When I went out to hit that same defensive back one time, he growled to me, 'You do that again, I'm going to mess you up,'" Hess said. "I kind of lifted my shoulders and spread my hands open and to the side saying, 'Alright, see you in a little bit.' A couple of plays later, I was on the left side on a running play, and I hit him again. He grabbed my jersey and pulled me in and punched me, and down we both went. "The referee came over, threw his flag, and announced, 'That's 15 yards, son. Unsportsmanlike conduct.' So, I helped the guy up and told him, 'Hey, you can punch me anytime you want. I'll take the 15 yards. I don't care.' They were trying to intimidate us, but by that time we were seasoned."

One of Duquesne's resident madmen, All-American linebacker John Stefanik, remembers putting his own brand of intimidation on display early in the Mattatuck contest. "There was a blitz, and I actually tackled the quarterback and the running back at the same time," he proudly reported. "I had one in one arm and one in the other arm, and I sacked them both. Then I looked down at the quarterback and gave him a Dukes' dose of aggression, 'Welcome to Pittsburgh. We're not done with you guys yet. We're just getting started.'"

Gridiron Dukes' running back Steve Sherer was also a target of Mattatuck's intimidation tactics. "Dan McCann knew we couldn't run the ball against them. So, we had a couple of formations where we had trips, and I was the inside receiver," Sherer revealed. "They put this linebacker on me who played like Jack Ham. The first time I lined up against him, he hit me with a flipper underneath my chin strap, and I couldn't swallow for about a quarter. But that motivated me. I was thinking, 'Somehow I have to get this guy back, somehow I have to show him something.'"

Midway through the second quarter, Mattatuck – which, you might remember, entered the game averaging nearly 30 points a matchup — set up for a field goal at the Duquesne 15-yard line, but the snap was high, and the contest remained scoreless.

Soon the Gridiron Dukes drove 68 yards in 11 plays, and Sherer got his revenge. After being hit in the throat, Steve approached Coach McCann on the sidelines and told him that he could beat "Jack Ham" on a swing pass. "And, thankfully, Dan listened to me," Sherer said. "So, we were lined up in trips, and I was the inside guy. I swung to the outside, and I got behind this linebacker. Davey Thomas hit me with a pass, and I went in and scored. That was my way of getting that guy back. But I must admit, I don't remember, before or after that Mattatuck game, ever getting hit as hard as I was that day. In fact, just talking about it, I can almost feel it!"

The 21-yard scoring strike down the right sideline from Thomas to Sherer came with 1:22 remaining before halftime. Shortly after that, Duquesne's Frank Hooper intercepted a pass and returned it 15 yards to the Mattatuck 42-yard line. I was in the booth with the Mt. Lebanon cable TV crew at that point as an expert on Duquesne's program. The cable play-by-play guy said, "Well, I guess Dan McCann is going to sit on the ball and take the lead into the locker room at halftime." Then he looked at Mt. Lebanon's color guy and said, "What do you think?" And the color guy confidently offered, "Oh yeah, this has been a tough game, and he's ahead 6-0. I'm sure that's what he'll do."

The play-by-play guy, in turn, looked at me quizzically, "What do you think, Sam?" My position was, "This is only the second time we've crossed the 50-yard line. I think Dan is going to throw a bomb to Rod Hess." And that's exactly what happened. On the next play, we threw that bomb to Rod, and he was wide open because Mattatuck, like the two men in the booth, also expected us to run the ball and let the clock run out. With 13 seconds left, Hess hauled in the touchdown pass from Thomas.

And guess what?

"The guy I burned for the touchdown was the one who told me that he was going to break my neck," Hess said with a smile. "McCann called, 'Flanker on the fly.' So, I just went straight. The guy did a bump-and-run with me. He was faster than I was, but I put a move on him and took off. I must have had the wind behind me or something, I don't know. But Davey Thomas threw a perfect pass. It came down right in my hands and ended up being the winning touchdown."

With the benefit of 2 TDs in a 69-second span, Duquesne held a 13-0 advantage at halftime — to the surprise of the many no doubt. The Gridiron Dukes had failed to convert a two-point conversion following the first touchdown, but Rich Sprys booted the extra point after the second TD.

In the third quarter, when Duquesne was having trouble mounting anything positive on offense, the president of the Allegheny County Police Association — Lt. James McGrath — approached Duquesne's publicist Tommy O'Malley. "I had been working with Lt. McGrath promoting the game," O'Malley explained. "We had this big trophy that had been purchased to give to the winning team. The lieutenant came up to me and cautioned me, 'Hey, you guys better get it going. I don't want this trophy going back to Connecticut.' I looked at Lt. McGrath and wondered exactly what he thought I could do — turn the dogs loose?" Everyone was feeling the pressure that day...

Mattatuck, which entered the game surrendering only 25.5 yards per game on the ground, had smartened up and then limited Sherer to 28 yards on 18 carries. Overall, Duquesne managed just 16 yards on 35 rushing attempts. However, Thomas completed 13 of 29 passes for 232 yards and both touchdowns. "He's a good quarterback with a real strong arm," McCann said of Thomas. "Remember, he had a full scholarship to Mississippi State before transferring here. That's the way we play football. We play it wide open from beginning to end."

Meanwhile, Dave Rossi of the Chiefs gained 171 yards on 25 carries and scored their only touchdown of the day on a 1-yard plunge with 4 minutes left in the contest. Remarkably, it was the first touchdown scored against Duquesne in the second half all season. A successful extra point made the score 13-7.

From the DU 27-yard line, Chiefs quarterback Larry Young tried to connect with Larry Walton near the front corner of the end zone. Walton and the Duke's McHenry leaped for the ball in unison, but McHenry outfought the Mattatuck receiver and came down with the interception as Mac's teammates jumped for joy.

In addition to seeing its championship hopes disappear, Mattatuck received 30 yards in penalties on the play for a personal foul and because its head coach, Dan Zaneski, ran onto the field in protest. "I was upset. The ball was in flight, and there was quite a bit of body contact," he told the Pittsburgh Press. "The rest was judgment. Some people were convinced that McHenry didn't have both feet in bounds, but that's judgment."

Those closing moments were packed with tension as Mattatuck had the ball and drove toward a touchdown that could have won the game if they were able to add the extra point. It took that heroic interception by safety Gary McHenry at the 2-yard line with 43 seconds left to secure the victory and clinch the National Title for Duquesne and win the Club Football National Championship/Children's Hospital Bowl at Three Rivers Stadium.

After the game, McHenry said, "Walton had been going down and out all day, and I was hoping they would throw it to him. I knew if they did, I would beat him."

"Mac saved the game for us. He really did," Hess said. "If he didn't do that, they would have scored, and we would have lost the game."

Our coach was flat-out far superior. Had Mattatuck attempted additional running plays with that big back they had, they would have won the game easily. They would have outscored the Gridiron Dukes. But their guy outcoached himself. They would give the ball to their big back, and he would get four yards. They would give the ball again to their big back, he would gain five yards. It would be third and one, and they would throw the ball, but we had better linebackers and a better secondary. We would knock the ball down or get to the quarterback almost every time.

Like everyone else, I saw the size advantage Mattatuck enjoyed. But it was also clear to me that the Gridiron Dukes had better skill players, linebackers and defensive backs. And even though Mattatuck's linemen had that tremendous size advantage, I felt Duquesne's linemen were smarter and quicker.

The Mattatuck Coach could not outduel the clever Dan McCann. Coach McCann baited the opponent into throwing the ball, and there, the Dukes had a distinct advantage.

Mattatuck threw the ball 24 times despite having a bulldozer in the backfield (Rossi). Young completed nine of those passes but was also picked off three times. Duquesne's Joe Alfier also had an interception to stop a Chiefs' drive in the fourth quarter. If we played them 10 times, we might have only won once. But the one time we played them, we won. That's what counted.

"To beat a team that's a lot bigger than you are, you need to play a smart game," added Hess, who caught 5 passes for 104 yards in the title game. "We were experienced. We had good technique.

We were well coached. And Mattatuck, well, those guys were just brute force. So, you need to work smarter not harder. That's what we did."

The 13-7 triumph that played out in front of 3,724 fans at Three Rivers Stadium was the first postseason victory for Duquesne since the Dukes defeated Mississippi State, 13-12, in the 1937 Orange Bowl.

"When you win a championship, there's nothing better. It stays with you your whole life," Duquesne tight end Terry Russell said. "Even though, like people said — and we used to get a bad rap all the time — 'You guys were just a Club Football Team.' Well, we were. But we were the best of the 80 Club Football Teams in the country. If you're the best at what you do, that's all that matters."

Stefanik has more than a few memories of that season, including the 'rinky-dink' comment by Coach McCann on his first day of practice. "After our win against Mattatuck, I went up to Dan and gave him a big hug, and said, 'How about those rinky-dink football players now, Coach?'" With a giant smile on his face, Dan replied, 'You can go find me all the rinky-dink football players you know.' Steve Sherer added, "It was then that I realized that Coach didn't mean anything by his rinky-dink comment that day, but he motivated all four of us, because we were definitely out to show him that we could play." Always with the motivation…

"You were growing up, life was good, and you just wanted to be a tough kid, and you wanted to play some football," Stefanik said. "The more we played together the closer and closer we got to each other, and we said, 'Let's finish this thing right. Let's go out as champions.' And we did. It was a great feeling."

DUQUESNE UNIVERSITY vs. MATTATUCK COMMUNITY COLLEGE

Club Football National Championship Game
Three Rivers Stadium – Pittsburgh, PA
November 20, 1973

SCORE BY QUARTERS

	1	2	3	4	FINAL
Mattatuck	0	0	0	7	7
Duquesne	0	13	0	0	13

SCORING PLAYS

DU: Steve Sherer 21-yard pass from Dave Thomas (conversion failed)

DU: Rod Hess 42-yard pass from Dave Thomas (Rich Sprys kick)

MCC: Dave Rossi 1-yard run (Don Newkirk kick)

TEAM STATS

	DU	MCC
First Downs	14	15
Rushing Yards	16	175
Passing Yards	232	126
Passes	13 for 30 (2 TD, 3 INT)	9 for 24 (0 TD, 3 INT)
Punts	6 (38.5 AVG)	8 (31.6 AVG)
Fumbles-Lost	1-1	1-1
Penalties-Yards	4 for 30	0 for 130

INDIVIDUAL STATS

RUSHING

DU: Sherer 18 carries for 28 yards; Mongillo 6 carries for 9 yards; Thomas 11 carries for -21 yards.

MCC: Marino 17 carries for 35 yards; Rossi 25 carries for 171 yards; Baden 1 carry for 6 yards; Newkirk 1 for -9; Young 3 for -15; Walton 1 for -13.

RECEIVING

DU: Hess 5 catches for 104 yards, 1 TD; Sherer 2 catches for 26 yards, 1 TD; DeMarco 2 catches for 64 yards; Mongillo 2 catches for 26 yards; Kresge 1 catch for -2 yards; Russell 1 catch for 14 yards.

MCC: Lee 1 catch for 17 yards; Terry 3 catches for 42 yards; Walton 5 catches for 67 yards.

ATTENDANCE — 3,724

15

CELEBRATION AT THE PILOT HOUSE... THEN GOLDSTEIN'S

AFTER THE ROUSING 13-7 VICTORY over Mattatuck Community College in the National Championship Game, there was a dinner party for both teams at a place called the Pilot House. It was a big boat that was docked along the Mon Wharf and had a really nice restaurant. Young men who had been bitter rivals on the football field hours earlier came together to break bread after gaining enormous respect for one another. Together they had staged an epic battle that no one on either side would ever forget.

"At the dinner that night, I was in line to get some food, and a Mattatuck kid came up to me and asked, 'Are you number 85?'" Rod Hess recalled. "I said, 'Yeah, I am.' He put out his hand to shake mine saying, 'Good game.' When he started to walk away, I put that same question to him, 'What number are you?' He replied, '25.' As it turned out, he ended up being the guy who said he was going to break my neck before I beat him for a touchdown."

Certainly, there were many interactions between Duquesne's Gridiron Dukes and Mattatuck's Chiefs on the boat that night that struck a far friendlier chord than what had transpired at Three Rivers Stadium. By about 12:30 a.m., the festivities at the Pilot House had concluded, and the Mattatuck squad headed back to its hotel. However, when you've just won a National Title, as Duquesne had, 12:30 a.m. was far too early to call it a night.

As the Gridiron Dukes began to exit the boat, Tommy O'Malley remembers Coach Dan McCann's saying to them, "I know where you're going, and I'm coming with you." Dan was referring to Goldstein's, a restaurant and bar that was located on Fifth Avenue near the foot of the Duquesne campus.

"A lot of our guys were a little bit older, and that was our hangout," O'Malley said. "Since Dan knew we were all going to Goldstein's, he and his wife, Rose, met all of us there and brought Chairman of the County Commissioners Tom Foerster with them. We got there and everyone was having a great time, then about 1:30 or so, the proprietor gave the "last call". And Dan immediately piped up with, 'Last call? We've got a championship football team here. Get us another keg of Iron City.' And, while the owner readily complied, cheers roared up from the excited crowd! It was at that point that Commissioner Foerster looked at us and said, 'Guys, it's time for me to go. Again, my hearty congratulations to you all.' He seemed to realize that we were going to be at Goldstein's for a while yet to celebrate our big win." After all, the Gridiron Dukes had earned it.

What was it like for the Duquesne Club Football Team when it finally sank in that they had captured the National Championship?

"It really was an all-night celebration," John Stefanik said. "We wanted to prove to the city of Pittsburgh that Club Football meant something. That's the thing that always irked me was the word 'club.' Mattatuck could have beaten a whole bunch of teams up and down the state. They could have beaten Waynesburg. They could have beaten CMU, and a lot of other teams that refused to play us.

That word 'club' was next to our name, but we could and would have stood up and played anybody.

Terry Russell remarked, "It was so exciting. How many times do you go 10-0? I used that later when I started coaching at Duquesne. When you're in a room, and you ask the players how many of them have won a championship, not too many hands go up. So, I used to say, 'Well, I'll tell you about a team I was on that won a championship. And this is how you do it, and these are the commitments that you have to make. To be the best, you have to do these things. If you're not willing to do them, then I think you need to pick another school to go to.'"

That was the standard of excellence established by the 1973 Gridiron Dukes.

16

PUBLICIZING DUQUESNE'S CLUB FOOTBALL TEAM
& TOM O'MALLEY

TOMMY O'MALLEY arrived on the Duquesne University campus in 1972, the year before the Gridiron Dukes won the National Championship, and during Dan McCann's third year as Head Coach.

Tommy came to Duquesne with publicity experience from working with the Pittsburgh Steelers, so it was with that know-how that, on Tuesday of each week, O'Malley would visit with McCann and then write a press release that recapped the previous week's game and provided a look ahead to the next matchup. On Thursdays, Tommy would deliver the latest news and information on DU football to the local TV stations, radio stations, and newspapers.

"Because my father worked at the (Pittsburgh) Press in advertising, I was familiar with the men who worked there. For the TV stations, because of my work with the Steelers, I knew most of those guys too. Because of these prior connections, we got some pretty good coverage. Ray Kienzl was the writer for the Press in charge of small college football. He would do a full article every week about Duquesne. I'd take my news release down, and then I'd have Dan call him if he had any questions. That was always nice.

"I'd also take releases out to Myron Cope, Billy Hillgrove, and Stan Savran at Channel 4, and I could walk right into Sam Nover's office at Channel 11. 'Tommy, you got more stuff on Duquesne?' he'd say. They were all great guys."

However, it was Vince Leonard, the hockey editor for the Pittsburgh Post-Gazette, who gave O'Malley some tough love — but he grew to appreciate those life-long lessons. Although Tommy was a journalism major at Duquesne, it was Vince who emphasized to O'Malley how important spelling, organization, and presentation were with regard to issuing successful press releases.

O'Malley's tireless work and his connections to the media helped create substantial awareness of the Duquesne Club Football Program. However, as any publicist can relate to, so did the team's achievements. Finishing 7-1 and third in the country in 1972 and going 9-0 on the way to the title game in 1973 piqued interest in the Gridiron Dukes.

After regular-season play concluded in 1973, Commissioner Foerster arranged for O'Malley to have access to office space at the County Courthouse where the young publicist promoted the National Championship Game — billed as the Children's Hospital Bowl — from there. "I'd go down to that office every day. Secretaries would help me produce very professional-looking releases which gave Duquesne a lot of good publicity.

"My news releases were finally organized, spelled properly, and had a great presentation too because one of the secretaries was helping me. We ended up getting a lot of good publicity. And I can remember taking (tackle) Jerry Kresge and (flanker) Rod Hess out to WTAE to be on Myron Cope's show the week before the game. There was quite a buzz around the Championship game."

Student publicity man, Tommy O'Malley was a tremendous asset to Duquesne's Gridiron Dukes Football Program.

17

PETE KULYK

HOW BASKETBALL TURNED TO FOOTBALL AND BACK AGAIN

PETE KULYK, the Director of the Duquesne Club Football Program during its inaugural season of 1969, came to the Bluff as a basketball player after starring at Archbishop Hoban High School in Akron, OH. Oh, and by the way, he grew up in the neighborhood that later produced NBA legend LeBron James.

After Pete led the Dukes' Freshman Basketball Squad in scoring, his sophomore and junior seasons were marred by knee and ankle injuries. That led to his stepping away from the basketball court and becoming involved with the football team.

"Since I wasn't involved in the basketball program anymore, Sam Costanzo came to me and asked, 'Would you be interested in getting involved with reviving football?'" Kulyk recalled. "And I said, 'Yeah, definitely.' Because in those days they didn't take away your scholarship. I'm walking around on campus on a full ride, but not really paying anything back. Football was an opportunity for me to pay back what the university was doing for me. So, I said, 'Yeah, whatever you need.' It was decided that I would be the first

Director of the Club Football Team, and I'll always feel grateful to Sam and the other guys who gave me that opportunity."

Kulyk graduated from Duquesne in the spring of 1970 then worked for some CPA firms and moved out to Arizona. Though his association with the Duquesne Football Program was rewarding, he often wondered what he could have accomplished in basketball had he remained healthy.

So, he did something about it.

"Eventually, what I did was — because I never got to do what I wanted to do basketball-wise in college because of my injuries — I went overseas and got contracts, and I wound up playing over there for 10 years," Kulyk said. "Nine of the 10 years were in France, and one was in Stockholm, Sweden. It really worked out great for me. I needed to play basketball when I got my health back. My knee came back, my ankle came back. I never intended to play 10 years overseas, but it was so much fun playing basketball and getting paid for it."

18

THROUGH THE EYES OF HIS DAUGHTER
VALERIE McCANN BUCEK

VALERIE McCANN BUCEK was 11 years old when her father led the Gridiron Dukes to the National Club Championship in 1973, but football was part of her life long before that.

"There's a picture of me on the wall in my house, I'm probably not even two years old," Valerie said. "I still have baby shoes on, and I'm standing there holding a football. I grew up with the game. I don't remember ever not understanding it. I remember people being surprised when I was really young and was watching games and standing on the sidelines."

For Dan and Rose McCann's only child, a long-time speech and language pathologist, football was an integral part of her family life. She remembers her mother typing up the playbook, and the ritual of putting those together in assembly-line fashion. "I still have some of those playbooks at my house. My dad kept one from every year." Valerie also recalls selling programs and lending a hand at the concessions stand at Stone Field in North

Park during Duquesne football games, and then helping to clean up afterward." For away games, bag lunches and meal money needed to be passed out.

In addition, early in Coach McCann's tenure at Duquesne, players would stop by the house to pick up equipment, and for many years he also hosted film study sessions with his assistant coaches.

"My dad would be at work (at Pittsburgh Brewing), so my grandfather and I (my mom's dad) would be at the house while the players came by and tried on their equipment," Valerie remembered. "You just had this handwritten sheet, and you checked guys off. The games were on Saturday, so my dad would watch the game films by himself on Sunday morning. On Sunday night, the coaches would come over to the house, and they would watch the films with him."

After hovering at the .500 mark for two seasons (4-3-1 in 1970 and 4-4 in 1971), Coach McCann shifted the program into high gear. Duquesne finished 7-1 and third in the club ranks in 1972 before roaring through the 1973 campaign with a perfect 10-0 record to capture the National Championship.

"Winning the National Championship gave the program validation, and the University recognized it," shared Valerie, who was on the sideline at Three Rivers Stadium for the 13-7 victory over Mattatuck Community College in that title game. "That '73 team did so well that people had to take notice. They were getting publicity in the newspapers, so the community was noticing them. That helped the program get financial support and made people want to come and see the games. It really boosted the program."

"My dad was very happy, very proud of the young men that he was mentoring. They had done well. He knew that they were going to continue to do well and that was going to help the program move forward. It was a wonderful season."

When Valerie matured and became more experienced, she realized that the Gridiron Dukes of the early 1970s were a special group of guys and not just because of their athletic ability and the success they enjoyed on the field. "Because they were a club group, they made their own travel arrangements, they made their own fundraising arrangements, they made a lot of their own decisions," she revealed. "I think because they were empowered like that they felt more of an investment in the team. That made them more collaborative with my father and, I think, more mature."

Coach McCann enjoyed all sports, but naturally football was his favorite. His daughter believes what made him successful during his career at Pittsburgh Brewing also made him an excellent coach. Namely, he was a salesman, and, as it has been identified by others in this book, he knew how to motivate people.

"I was very much wrapped up in my dad's success," Valerie recalled. "When he won, I always made sure I was one of the first people to run on to the field to hug him and congratulate him. And I also wanted to be one of the first ones to be out there if he lost to be supportive.

"My dad was larger than life. He was a big guy, and he had a big heart. One of the things he'd say all the time was, 'It's a great day to be alive.' And that's what he'd say after he won a game too. 'Gentlemen, it's a great day to be alive.' And he lived his life that way."

19

BORN WITH DUQUESNE IN HIS BLOOD
JUDGE JACK MCVAY

JACK MCVAY has incredible passion for Duquesne University and its football program, and he came by that honestly. Not only were both his father and mother Duquesne graduates but also he and his wife, Janine, as well.

Jack attended Sunday Mass at St. Therese in Munhall with his family, as a kid, and there happened to be an usher that Jack's dad pointed out to him. McVay said his dad told him, "That guy there is Boyd Brumbaugh, who was a star for the Dukes in the 1930s. He was a great football player at Duquesne when they went to the Orange Bowl."

Brumbaugh was an outstanding player for the 1936 Dukes that went 8-2 and handed Pitt its only loss as the Panthers went on to capture the National Title that season. In the 1937 Orange Bowl, it was Brumbaugh's 72-yard halfback pass to Ernie Hefferle late in the game that lifted Duquesne to a thrilling 13-12 triumph over Mississippi State.

During the summer of 1972, before McVay's junior year at Bishop Boyle High School, he was at preseason camp with the football team at South Park Fairgrounds, and Duquesne's Club Football Squad was working out there too. "They were at one end of the grounds, and my high school team was at the other end," Jack said. "That was when I got my first exposure to the fact that Duquesne had a football team."

McVay's senior year, as a quarterback for Bishop Boyle, came in 1973, which was also when the Gridiron Dukes went undefeated and won the National Title. "During my senior year, I received letters from a lot of Presidents' Conference schools, but at the same time Duquesne's team was getting all kinds of local media exposure for winning games, playing at Three Rivers Stadium, going undefeated, and ultimately winning the National Championship. In the end, what I was seeing and hearing about the Dukes sealed the deal for me."

When Jack got to Duquesne in the fall of 1974, Coach Dan McCann told him that his days as a quarterback were over — after just one scrimmage. "He took a look at my blazing speed and decided that I should become an offensive lineman," McVay good-naturedly shared. "I got moved pretty quickly, but I just wanted to play. I told Dan and "Pro," 'If that's what you want, then that's what I'll do.'"

Toward the end of his freshman season, Jack became a starter at guard. Then for the next three years he started at center and became a two-time All-American. Duquesne went 7-2 and made it back to the Club Football National Championship game when McVay was a senior in 1977. However, the Iron Dukes (as they had become known by then) lost, 41-6, to UMass-Lowell in that contest. "Sometimes it bothers me that it's hardly ever mentioned that we made it to the National Championship game that year too,"

Jack said. "But we got beat pretty good. UMass-Lowell had a really good team."

At Duquesne, Jack went on to earn a Pharmacy Degree in 1980 and a Law Degree in 1984. He's currently a Judge in the Civil Division of the Allegheny County Court of Common Pleas, and he's still an avid follower of Duquesne football.

In 2014, McVay was elected to the Duquesne Sports Hall of Fame. During his acceptance remarks, he talked about how important the University and its football program have been to him and what the 1973 National Championship team meant to him. "I look back at my life, and I owe so much to Duquesne. I really feel that way," he said. "I'm a pharmacist and a judge. That's all because of Duquesne. But I decided to go here because of the football program. Duquesne is in my blood."

20

A TIP OF THE CAP FROM HEAD COACH JERRY SCHMITT

JERRY SCHMITT has built an impressive resume highlighted by his long run as Head Football Coach of the Duquesne Dukes – a run that reached 20 seasons in 2024. During that period, the team compiled a 128-86 record (60% winning), was conference champion or co-champion 10 times, and made 3 trips to the NCAA Football Championship Series (FCS) playoffs. Duquesne enjoyed a winning season 15 times in those 20 years, and Schmitt was named conference coach or co-coach of the year on 4 occasions.

He's well decorated now, but his first opportunity to coach in the college ranks came in 1985 when he was 25 years old, and Terry Russell put him in charge of the Defensive Line at Duquesne. Russell, one of the stars of the university's 1973 National Championship Squad, was the Head Coach of the Dukes at that time.

"Terry is the uncle of a really good friend who happened to be a college teammate of mine at Westminster, so I knew of Terry, and Terry knew of me," Schmitt said. "He needed a Line Coach, so I joined his staff. From that point on, I was able to meet a number of the guys from the National Championship Team, learn about the history, and gain an appreciation for what occurred at that time. It was pretty cool to hear how the program came together back then."

Schmitt was an Assistant under three different head coaches at Duquesne — Russell (1985-87), Dan McCann (1992) and Greg Gattuso (1993-99). That being the case, he's well versed on how the program evolved from a Club Team to Division III to I-AA Non-Scholarship and finally to I-AA Scholarship. What's more, Schmitt doesn't think it's too dramatic to suggest that none of that would have happened had it not been for the men who started the Club Team in 1969.

"There's truth to the fact that we have no idea where Duquesne Football would be at this point — despite the growth of the program and the success that we've had here — without that group of guys," Schmitt said. "Without guys like Sam Costanzo and Dan McCann, who brought the program back and won a National Championship within five years, you just don't know what would have happened."

Schmitt makes a point to familiarize his players with the rags-to-riches story of the Duquesne Club Football Program. Sammy DeMarco, a standout receiver on the '73 squad, is a cousin of Schmitt's Offensive Coordinator, Anthony Doria. One time when DeMarco sat in on a team meeting, Schmitt introduced him to the squad, presented him with a team jersey, and the players gave DeMarco a standing ovation that genuinely moved him. "Coach Doria told me that Sammy said it was one of the highlights of his career," Schmitt said. "I try to do stuff like that all the time because of the tradition those guys started. I tell our kids about it all the time."

In early April of 2024, when the Duquesne Football Team received its championship rings for winning the 2023 NEC title at a banquet on campus, a dozen or so members of the 1973 team were there to witness the moment — at Schmitt's gracious invitation.

Schmitt said he never tires of hearing stories from the guys who were part of the Club Football Program in that 1969-to-1973 window. In February of 2024, he was invited to Shale's Cafe by Tommy O'Malley after a Duquesne basketball game at the UPMC Cooper Fieldhouse. O'Malley held court at Shale's for nearly three hours that day telling story after story — which he's really good at by the way.

"I've heard many, many of the stories, and I still just enjoy them," Schmitt says. "I've gotten to know Rod Hess. And I'm good friends with Sam Costanzo and Timmy Kelly, who played on that ('73) team. His brother was my Offensive Coordinator when I was the Head Coach at Westminster. Sammy DeMarco, I played flag football with right out of college.

"Dan McCann, too. It's been well documented how much he did for the program. He and I developed a friendship, and I've gotten a lot of the program's history from him. From when I took over until his passing, Dan continued to have a big impact on the program and me. He was very supportive.

"I have great respect for those guys and great appreciation for how they've supported Duquesne Football and me through the years. Even outside of my role and position here, I'm interested personally because I'm from Pittsburgh. Football is big in this town, and what those guys did is part of our history here. I just think it's an outstanding story."

AFTERWORD
BY DAVE HARPER

AS A FORMER COLLEGE FOOTBALL COACH and the current Athletic Director at Duquesne, I have a profound appreciation of foundations. When I say that, I mean that all programs have a point where they have been established or reestablished to build the foundation upon which things can be grown for success. As I learned of Duquesne football being rebuilt from the ground up via club football, to non-scholarship football, and now playing at the FCS level, I certainly can appreciate all of the past players, coaches, supporters, and leaders who made our program championship caliber.

It is hard to fathom the challenge of establishing not only the basics to run a program, but the additional challenge of building a winning culture. I will tell you that two of the key staples needed to build culture are passion and competitiveness. When I first met Sam Costanzo, Dan McCann, and others responsible for the rebirth of Duquesne football, the passion they exuded was apparent from the first moment. Their pride, their person, all clearly indicated that a winning football program was going to thrive regardless of challenges.

Today our program is playing on national television, winning conference championships, assisting in building the university's brand nationally, and graduating driven learners, competitors and leaders. All of it is possible due to the foundation built from the rebirth of football at Duquesne. As a father of four boys who all played football on the collegiate level, I can attest to the lessons learned being a part of a team, and respect the opportunities created for the players and the team. I have a deep appreciation for where we are today and why it is possible. At Duquesne, we must continue to be stewards of the program and assure its long-term sustainability and success with a deep appreciation for its roots.

DAVE HARPER
Vice President of Athletics
Duquesne University

ACKNOWLEDGEMENTS
BY SAM COSTANZO

WRITING THIS BOOK on the rich and storied history of Duquesne Club Football has been a journey made possible by the support, expertise, and enthusiasm of many individuals and institutions. I am deeply grateful to all those who have contributed in various ways to this endeavor.

A special thank you to Duquesne University's current President, Ken Gormley, whose exceptional leadership and scholarly guidance ensure and promote the continued excellence of our University. Thank you also to his staff for their contributions to ensuring the accuracy of this historical compilation.

There are so many individuals who played pivotal roles in making the return of Club Football possible. Each of their contributions was critical and, without any one of them, our venture may very well have failed. My gratitude to these pioneers cannot be overstated.

To Jim Lachimia, thank you for investing time and efforts and conducting the original interviews for this story. I also extend my heartfelt thanks to Gina Samosky for her unwavering perseverance and invaluable support in editing and refining this work.

And to my dear friend, Dick Roberts. His profound professionalism, keen eye, and thoughtful suggestions significantly shaped the final manuscript.

Thank you to Frank Trunzo, who first whispered the idea of Club Football into the ear of Father McNamara, just a whisper which became the genesis of our program.

I would also like to thank Pete Kulyk, the Co-Founder of our Club and our First Director. His friendship and perseverance were essential as we navigated the challenges of launching this new venture. Fun fact: He took a shot at playing quarterback during one preseason practice, but quickly chose to focus on his collegiate and later professional basketball career.

*Reverend Henry J. McAnulty, ninth President of the University, who was our greatest supporter for starting our Program.

*Pete Dimperio, whose sage advice and consultation as a mentor and one of the best coaches in Western Pennsylvania's history, was invaluable.

*Ken Curcio, my college roommate, whose assistance at the beginning was critical to our success and has been instrumental in piecing together the intricate tapestry of Duquesne Club Football's past. His memories and recall of these incredible years have been an invaluable resource. His advice, support, and, most of all, his fervent loyalty, remain with me to this very day.

*Bob Grochowski, who kept the Club Football Team afloat all those year ago, and 56 years later is still the most brilliant CPA that I have met. He's a tough guy with a big heart. He has guided us through some rough waters, and I am eternally grateful.

*Bob Skoff, who succeeded me in running our Program and ensuring its continued success.

*Lou Grenci, the Duquesne Dukes Football Program's original stat man.

*John "Skitch" Henderson, our first trainer who taped up each member of the team for all practices and games and kept us entertained with his comical caricatures over his years at Duquesne.

*Rita Joyce, President of Student Congress at that time, who strongly supported our Football Program and made a financial commitment from that student organization.

*Valerie McCann Bucek for supporting Duquesne football and her father's lifelong passion for the sport. She was his No. 1 assistant at home while he was Head Coach and went on to organize his Pittsburgh Coaches Corner Luncheons for decades. Having her by his side through it all was one of his greatest joys.

*Joe Nicoletti, our first Coach, who led the way for future success.

Thank you to each of the club's participants and supporters who generously shared their personal stories and perspectives adding depth and authenticity to the account. Their firsthand experiences and memories have brought the history of Duquesne Club Football to life in ways I could not have imagined alone.

To the members of the infamous 13th floor of St. Martin's Hall including among others Harry Dudro, Lou Grenci, Hugh McGinnis, Gary McHenry, Jon Neiderer, Joe Sabol, Dave Sirhal, Rick "Spinny" Spinhoven, and Jim Vumbaco. Whether they worked the chains, delivered checks to cover the opposing team's expenses, hit the gridiron with unwavering intensity, or provided other critical support, they are the reason we successfully brought football back to our esteemed University.

I also want to acknowledge my 1969 teammates some of whom should have been All-Americans had they gotten the recognition they deserved.

I would like to express my gratitude to Terry Russell whose versatility on the field was unmatched. He played nearly every position — including quarterback, tight end, center, and flanker. In addition to his playing career, Terry has contributed as both an Assistant Coach and Head Coach. He was honored as Duquesne University's Athlete of the Year in 1974 and was inducted into the University's Sports Hall of Fame in 1993 and the Western Pennsylvania Sports Hall of Fame in 2024. Terry's dedication was instrumental in keeping Duquesne Football alive.

And finally, to Coach Dan McCann, without whom there would be no Duquesne University Football today, and certainly no 1973 Club National Championship. While I regret that he did not get to see this project completed, I will cherish his friendship and influence in my life forever. This book is a tribute to his passion and dedication.

Thank you all for being a part of this journey and for helping to bring the story of football's history to life.

— Sam Costanzo

WA

www.ingramcontent.com/pod-product-compliance
Lightning Source LLC
Chambersburg PA
CBHW070106080526
44586CB00013B/1203